ADRIANA LUNA CARLOS

Editor-In-Chief, Designer
and Co-Founder

HANNA OLIVAS

Managing Editor
& Co-Founder

NICOLE CURTIS

Director of the SRS
Magazine Division

VITALITY DIGEST

**ADVERTISING
OPPORTUNITIES**

Info@SheRisesStudios.com

**VITALITY DIGEST MAGAZINE
OCTOBER 2024**

**SHE RISES
STUDIOS**

CONTACT US

SheRisesStudios@gmail.com
www.SheRisesStudios.com

www.SheRisesStudios.com

LETTER FROM THE EDITORS

Dear Readers,

Welcome to the October 2024 edition of Vitality Digest Magazine!

As fall settles in, we're excited to bring you an issue filled with renewal, wellness, and inspiration. This season is the perfect time to reflect on your personal journey and reconnect with your body, mind, and soul. Our cover story features Melissa Ferrer-Burke, whose incredible work in healing through art and holistic wellness is transforming lives. Her dedication to empowering women through creative expression and community shines throughout this issue.

In addition to Melissa's inspiring story, we're offering a special sneak peek inside the FENIX TV Luxury Gifting Suite during Emmys Week! Get an exclusive look at the luxurious and health-conscious products that celebrities received, as well as how wellness continues to influence Hollywood. We're blending a touch of glamor with practical, enriching advice to elevate your fall experience.

This edition also brings you nourishing fall recipes and wellness tips to help you thrive as the season changes. From art therapy to mindful practices, our goal is to equip you with tools to heal, grow, and maintain balance during this time of transition. Nourishing your soul this fall is not just about self-care, but about embracing the possibilities of transformation.

We hope this issue inspires you to embrace fall with open arms and an open heart. With stories of empowerment, luxury sneak peeks, and expert wellness advice, this edition of Vitality Digest is your guide to thriving as you nurture your soul, one mindful step at a time.

Warm regards,

Adriana Luna Carlos and Hanna Olivas
Editors of Vitality Digest Magazine

SHE RISES STUDIOS

FENIX TV

EMPOWER**HER** CONTENT DAY

at

Elevate Your Brand Through Creative And Impactful Content!

EmpowerHer Content Day equips attendees with the tools and knowledge needed to craft compelling content for social media, podcasts, and videos.

FEBRUARY 22, 2025

TOTAL ACCESS TICKET: $127

WWW.SHERISESSTUDIOS.COM

MELISSA FERRER-BURKE: EMPOWERING WOMEN THROUGH ART AND HEALING AT ELLEVATE HER

by Melissa Ferrer-Burke

In a world where art meets healing, Melissa Ferrer-Burke stands as a visionary leader, passionately dedicated to empowering women through the transformative power of creative expression. As the CEO and "Visionary-in-Chief" of **Ellevate Her**, a healing center and foundation launched in 2023, Melissa has cultivated a sanctuary for women to thrive, offering programs that focus on recovery, self-discovery, and personal growth. With a lifetime of personal experience and artistic exploration, Melissa has crafted an environment where art, therapy, and holistic wellness come together to foster healing for single women.

Melissa's journey is one marked by resilience and the determination to turn her personal experiences into something meaningful for others. A trauma survivor herself, she is no stranger to the complexities of healing, and it is this profound understanding that drives her commitment to supporting women on their paths to recovery. *"I passionately believe in the transformative power of the arts to empower women. Throughout my life, I have dedicated myself to supporting women, channeling my own experiences and artistic vision into meaningful action,"* she explains.

The Creation of Ellevate Her: A Lifelong Vision Realized
In the fall of 2023, Melissa launched **Ellevate Her**, a foundation based in Florida that is more than just a center for healing; it is a sanctuary where women can come together in a nurturing community to learn, grow, and express themselves. For Melissa, the timing of the foundation's launch was deeply personal and symbolic. She attributes much of the center's creation to what she refers to as *"divine timing,"* where all of her life's experiences, education, and global exposure

came together at the right moment to serve others. *"All of my life's experiences and education were able to come together at this time to help others along their healing paths,"* she says, reflecting on the foundation's beginnings.

A Lifetime of Learning and Mentorship
Melissa's journey to becoming a leader in healing and empowerment didn't happen overnight. She acknowledges the importance of mentorship and guidance in her life, having studied healing programs, wellness retreats, and artistic workshops around the world. Each of these experiences was pivotal in shaping the programs offered at **Ellevate Her**. From art therapy to yoga, breathwork, and even cold plunging, every modality has been personally explored by Melissa on her own path to healing. *"Every program we offer at EH I have personally studied, used, and found helpful along my personal journey,"* she shares. This hands-on approach ensures that the women at **Ellevate Her** receive authentic, effective support.

Art as a Path to Healing
At the heart of **Ellevate Her** lies the belief that art can be a powerful tool for healing. The center offers a variety of art therapy sessions designed to provide women with a safe space to express their emotions without the need for words. *"Art therapy can provide a safe environment for authentic expression, an opportunity to 'verbalize' inner emotions without having to talk, can help contain overwhelming emotions, and help reconcile negative feelings,"* Melissa explains. The creative process allows women to connect with their innermost selves, using artistic expression as a means of self-discovery and emotional healing.

The "Rise, Melissa" Art Series: A Collaborative Journey of Transformation

Melissa's personal journey of resilience and empowerment is perhaps most vividly captured in her art series, **"Rise, Melissa."** This collection of six artworks is a collaborative effort between Melissa and world-renowned photographer Robert Farber, with whom she has shared both a personal and professional relationship for over 25 years. Their creative partnership, which began in 1999, has produced a body of work that seamlessly blends photography and painting to tell a compelling narrative of transformation.

"Combining my true emotion and his elegant lens, we were able to connect sight and feeling as subject and photographer," Melissa reflects on the collaboration. The **"Rise, Melissa"** series takes viewers on a powerful journey of growth, resilience, and self-discovery, using vivid colors and evocative imagery to convey the emotional experiences Melissa has encountered throughout her life.

Building a Community of Empowerment

While art is central to the work at **Ellevate Her**, Melissa believes that the true strength of the foundation lies in its community. "You're only as strong as your team. In one word, community," she emphasizes. The center is designed to be a supportive environment where women can heal and grow together. The women at **Ellevate Her** come from diverse backgrounds, but they are united by a shared mission of healing and empowerment.

The success of the foundation's programs is a testament to Melissa's holistic approach. Whether it's through art therapy, life coaching, or physical practices like yoga and breathwork, the programs at **Ellevate Her** are tailored to each individual. *"Each individual is unique. We at EH are proud to say that we cater programs to each specific case,"* Melissa explains. This personalized approach has led to life-changing transformations for many of the women who have participated.

The Power of Collaboration and Knowledge Sharing

For Melissa, collaboration is key to creating a thriving community. She believes that every woman has unique skills and experiences to offer, and that by learning from one another, they can become stronger. *"Knowledge is power. We all have such a unique set of skills. We learn from each other and are always stronger together and united,"* she says.

Melissa's dedication to this philosophy extends beyond the walls of **Ellevate Her**. She envisions the foundation as a global movement, connecting women from around the world who share a common goal of healing and personal expansion. Already, she is working to bridge her home base in South Florida with Florence, Italy, providing opportunities for international education and collaboration.

Looking to the Future

As **Ellevate Her** continues to grow, Melissa's vision for the future is expansive. *"I see EH building centers globally,"* she says, envisioning a network of healing centers that empower women worldwide. Her goal is to create spaces where women can connect, heal, and learn from one another, transcending geographical boundaries to build a global sisterhood of support and empowerment.

Through her unwavering dedication, Melissa Ferrer-Burke is not only transforming the lives of the women she serves, but also demonstrating the profound impact that art and community can have on the healing process. **Ellevate Her** is a reflection of her life's work—an ongoing journey of resilience, empowerment, and creativity that continues to inspire women to rise to their fullest potential.

CONNECT WITH MELISSA

www.instagram.com/ellevate_her
www.linkedin.com/company/ellevate-her/about
www.ellevateher.org

Photo Credits: Rosina Di Bello
@rosinadibellophoto

OCTOBER'S EMBRACE

by Hanna Olivas

October's here, a crisp, cool breeze,
The world turns gold with rustling leaves.
It's time to wrap in cozy hues,
And let the magic gently fuse.

Pumpkin spice and evening glow,
Where dreams ignite and passions grow.
October whispers, "Take your chance,"
In every leaf, a daring dance.

For me, this month is more than fall,
It's where I heed my heart's true call.
To chase my dreams with fearless grace,
And carve new paths in every space.

I find my strength in autumn's light,
In darker days, my vision's bright.
October is my time to soar,
To build, to thrive, to love, explore.

So here's to all who feel the flame,
Who seek to play October's game.
Let's make this month a canvas wide,
And paint our lives with joy and pride.

HEALING REGRET WITH COMPASSION AND EMDR

by Shari B. Kaplan, LCSW

"The root cause of regret is the belief that had you had made a different choice that somehow life would be better."

It has been well studied that most regrets revolve around finances, education, career, parenting, intimate relationships, and self improvement.

According to Daniel Pink's book Power of regret, there are 4 types of regret.

- Foundational regret which are regrets around education, finances and health.
- Boldness regret, which are regrets concerning opportunities that are missed by not making brave choices and playing it safe,
- Moral regrets which involve a lack of judgment that does not align with your personal ethics.
- Connection regrets which involve how you behaved in relationships whether you neglected them or didn't connect soon enough.

When we have unresolved regret it is because we have not to our choices and ourselves from a perspective of compassion. We are holding ourselves hostage to the belief that we have done something bad or we are something bad.

A healthy relationship to regret would be:

- Looking at the choices that you made, recognizing that those choices were hurtful, or painful,
- Take responsibility for the choices, understanding that being human is about figuring out how to do life on planet Earth, we all make mistakes.
- Understanding that from those choices you can make better choice in your life moving forward

Having said that, many people get stuck on *'I did something bad and I am powerless to fix it,'* or 'I am something bad' and I'll never be able to trust myself to make good choices moving forward.

These types of root causes beliefs of being powerless or or believing that you can't trust yourself, causes your body to stay in a state of fight flight or freeze, which is our survival instinct. This can either paralyze you from moving forward or keep you in a chronic state of hyperarousal. When you are in height and state of hyperarousal, your vagus nerve is being stressed, because your body is getting the message that it is under constant attack in this case, you are attacking yourself with these negative beliefs. This can cause a cascade of medical issues, including chronic pain, obsessive thinking, sleeplessness, anxiety, depression, attention deficits, and OCD.

As with most things in life, we can either change our situation or change the way we relate to our situation. When it comes to regret, our only choices are to change the way we relate to the situation and how we choose to behave as we move forward.

Compassion based therapy using EMDR and other experiential modalities of therapy such as internal family systems can be extremely helpful in repairing the root cause of the negative beliefs. Believing you are bad, you've done something bad or you are powerless and untrustworthy will take a little bit more than positive self talk to correct when you are stuck in those beliefs. EMDR and internal family systems helps to target where the beliefs live in your body and mind. EMDR targets Beliefs, feelings, emotions (where feelings are experienced in

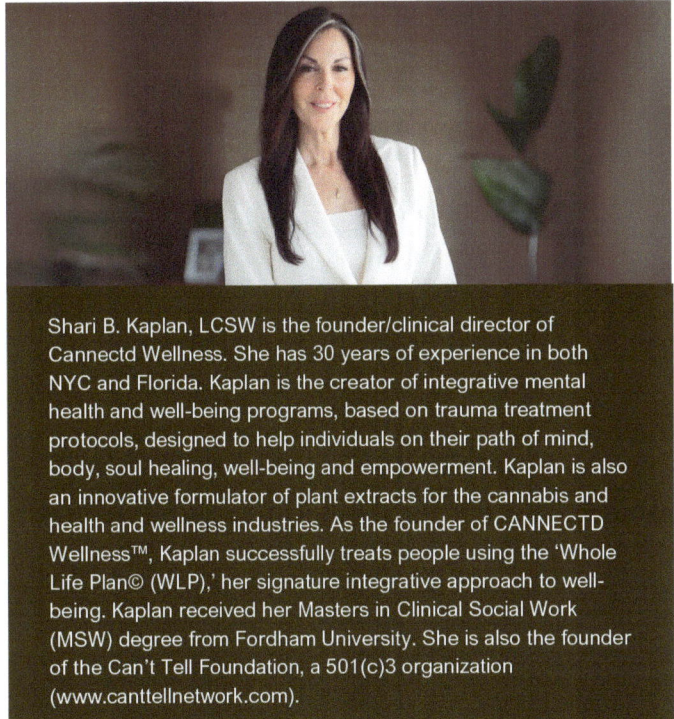

Shari B. Kaplan, LCSW is the founder/clinical director of Cannectd Wellness. She has 30 years of experience in both NYC and Florida. Kaplan is the creator of integrative mental health and well-being programs, based on trauma treatment protocols, designed to help individuals on their path of mind, body, soul healing, well-being and empowerment. Kaplan is also an innovative formulator of plant extracts for the cannabis and health and wellness industries. As the founder of CANNECTD Wellness™, Kaplan successfully treats people using the 'Whole Life Plan© (WLP),' her signature integrative approach to well-being. Kaplan received her Masters in Clinical Social Work (MSW) degree from Fordham University. She is also the founder of the Can't Tell Foundation, a 501(c)3 organization (www.canttellnetwork.com).

your body as tension or anxiety) and thoughts and helps to release them from your mind and body, then helps to re-organize your beliefs with compassion and in healthy beliefs. with more compassionate, empowering beliefs you can get unstuck and move forward with a healthier way of looking at the past choices that you were making. As Maya Angelo says, *'when we know better we do better.'*

It is easier to develop compassion for yourself in the face of a loving compassionate individual who could support you through the process of reframing your past mistakes or decisions and how to move forward, making choices that are more in alignment with your beliefs and values. Having an awareness that it is part of the human condition to learn and grow as we are taking this journey through life on planet earth.

Regrets can go away if you are able to explore

- why you made the choices you made,
- understanding that you did the best you could with where you were at,
- develop a belief that when you know better you do better,
- regret is a universal experience for everyone on this planet so we can reflect on past choices and say I could've done that differently.
- being able to acknowledge your strengths and all of the choices that you do make in your life that have led to positive outcomes.
- Understanding the choices that you made were out of fear and that was valid at that time , and you can choose differently now moving forward." – Shari B. Kaplan, LCSW

REBECCA CHANDLER: HEALING HEARTS AND BODIES

Rebecca Chandler's life journey is a testament to the power of resilience, healing, and the transformative potential of holistic wellness practices. As a survivor of infant and teenage abuse, Rebecca's path to healing was marked by decades of chronic illness, pain, and emotional turmoil. Yet, through her unwavering determination and commitment to holistic healing, Rebecca emerged as a beacon of hope and inspiration for countless individuals seeking a path to wellness.

In her chapter, *"Moving the Mountains in Your Heart,"* Rebecca shares profound insights into the Eastern perspective on the heart as the benevolent ruler of the body—an organ system deeply intertwined with one's physical, emotional, and spiritual well-being. Drawing from her own experiences and the wisdom of Traditional Chinese Medicine (TCM), Rebecca illuminates the intricate connections between heart health, vitality, and overall wellness.

At the heart of Rebecca's healing journey lies the Wholistic 5-part healing system—an integrative approach to wellness that addresses the physical, emotional, and spiritual dimensions of health. Through practices such as colon hydrotherapy, herbal detoxification, and nourishing whole foods, Rebecca embarked on a journey of cellular cleansing and renewal, paving the way for profound healing and transformation.

Central to Rebecca's healing journey is the recognition of the interconnectedness between physical health and spiritual well-being. Through her faith and spiritual practice, Rebecca discovered a profound source of love, inspiration, and healing—a revelation that underscored the importance of nurturing the spirit as a cornerstone of true wellness.

As Rebecca shares her journey of healing and self-discovery, she offers invaluable insights and practical tools for individuals seeking to embark on their own path to wellness. From the importance of purifying the blood to the transformative power of serving others, Rebecca's wisdom serves as a guiding light for those navigating their own journey of healing and transformation.

Through her work at the Wholistic Arizona Healing Ranch, Rebecca and her husband, Ron, have created a sanctuary for healing and renewal—a place where individuals and families can find solace, support, and holistic care. With compassion, expertise, and a deep commitment to healing, Rebecca continues to empower others to reclaim their health, vitality, and joy.

Rebecca Chandler's journey is a testament to the resilience of the human spirit and the transformative power of holistic healing. Through her unwavering dedication to wellness, Rebecca embodies the spirit of hope, resilience, and empowerment, inspiring others to embark on their own journey of healing and transformation.

CONNECT WITH REBECCA

www.linkedin.com/in/rebecca-chandler-80207b229
www.facebook.com/rebecca.chandler.585
www.twitter.com/wholisticaz
www.wholisticarizona.com
www.wholisticarizona.com/wholisticfinance

PRIORITIZE SELF-CARE TO THRIVE: INSIGHTS FROM JENNIFER & NATASHA

by Jennifer Griffith and Natasha Ganes

In today's fast-paced world, stress has become an unavoidable part of life. However, prolonged stress can lead to burnout, affecting our mental, physical, and emotional well-being. Jennifer Griffith and Natasha Ganes, co-creators of "In the Life of Zen" and hosts of the "Where Money Meets Soul" podcast, understand the importance of prioritizing self-care to avoid burnout and thrive in every aspect of life.

Drawing from their combined expertise in health, wellness, and professional development, Jennifer and Natasha offer valuable insights into the transformative power of self-care. Through their own personal journeys, they have discovered the profound impact that prioritizing self-care can have on overall well-being.

Natasha's Story resonates with many individuals who find themselves juggling multiple responsibilities and struggling to manage stress effectively. As a busy woman with numerous commitments, Natasha understands the challenges of balancing career, family, and personal goals. At one point, stress consumed her life, leaving her overwhelmed and exhausted. However, through prioritizing self-care, Natasha was able to regain control of her life and find fulfillment.

Similarly, Jennifer's Story highlights the dangers of neglecting self-care in pursuit of productivity. As someone who thrives on constant activity and achievement, Jennifer found herself on the brink of burnout after years of relentless work. Recognizing the importance of self-care, Jennifer embarked on a journey of self-discovery and transformation, reclaiming her health and happiness in the process.

Stress, overwhelm, and burnout are common experiences in today's society, but Jennifer and Natasha emphasize the importance of recognizing the signs and taking proactive steps to prioritize self-care. By incorporating self-care practices into daily routines, individuals can protect their mental and physical health, enhance productivity, and cultivate a greater sense of well-being.

To avoid burnout and thrive in life, Jennifer and Natasha offer practical tips for prioritizing self-care:

1. **Write Down Everything You Need to Do and Learn to Delegate:** By creating a list of tasks and prioritizing them, individuals can identify areas where they can delegate or eliminate tasks that are not essential.
2. **Accept Your Emotions and Change Your Perspective:** Instead of dwelling on negative thoughts and emotions, practice gratitude and focus on positive aspects of life.

3. **Create Boundaries and Stick with Them:** Learn to say no to commitments that are not aligned with your priorities, and establish healthy boundaries to protect your time and energy.
4. **Exercise:** Incorporate regular physical activity into your routine to reduce stress, boost mood, and improve overall health.
5. **Practice Mindfulness:** Take time to quiet the mind and focus on the present moment through meditation, deep breathing, or other mindfulness practices.
6. **Try Something New:** Step out of your comfort zone and engage in activities that bring joy and fulfillment, whether it's learning a new hobby or exploring new experiences.
7. **Take a Digital Detox:** Disconnect from electronic devices periodically to reduce screen time and promote relaxation.
8. **Meditate:** Set aside time for meditation or guided relaxation to calm the mind and reduce stress.
9. **Prioritize Sleep:** Ensure adequate rest by establishing a bedtime routine and creating a conducive sleep environment.

By incorporating these self-care practices into daily life, individuals can protect their well-being, enhance resilience, and unlock their full potential. Jennifer and Natasha's message is clear: prioritizing self-care is not selfish; it's essential for living a balanced, fulfilling life.

Through their platform, "In the Life of Zen," Jennifer and Natasha share their experiences and insights to empower others to prioritize self-care and create the life of their dreams. By embracing self-care as a non-negotiable aspect of life, individuals can cultivate greater happiness, resilience, and overall well-being.

In the journey of life, self-care is the key to unlocking our full potential and living with purpose and passion. With Jennifer and Natasha's guidance, individuals can embark on a transformative journey of self-discovery, empowerment, and holistic well-being.

CONNECT WITH JENNIFER AND NATASHA

www.instagram.com/inthelifeofzen
www.facebook.com/inthelifeofzen
www.linkedin.com/company/53218206/admin
www.inthelifeofzen.com

EMMYS WEEK: A JOURNEY FROM LAS VEGAS TO HOLLYWOOD

It all began with a drive from Las Vegas to Hollywood—a journey filled with anticipation and excitement as my daughter, a team member, and I hit the road. The promise of Emmys Week loomed ahead, and we couldn't wait to immerse ourselves in the magic that awaited us. Our hearts raced at the thought of the extraordinary people we would meet and the unforgettable experiences that lay in store.

Upon our arrival at the hotel, the atmosphere was electric. We were greeted by smiling faces, and the energy in the air was palpable. As we set up our space, I took a moment to soak in the scene. The room buzzed with life as we prepared to host some of the most celebrated figures in the entertainment industry. It felt like stepping into a different era—a revival of that old Hollywood charm characterized by kindness, generosity, and genuine connection.

Photo Credit: Jared Leighton

Listening to the beats of the DJ set the tone for the evening, creating an ambiance that was both inviting and exhilarating. The extraordinary talent on display, from our featured performers to the dazzling array of sponsors showcasing their incredible products, transformed the night into a celebration of creativity and collaboration. Influencers, bloggers, and celebrities mingled under the stars, creating an atmosphere that was nothing short of magical.

W Hollywood Hotel, with its stunning views and rich history, served as the perfect backdrop for this enchanting experience. Its beauty made everything feel surreal, as if we had stepped into a dream. I couldn't help but reflect on how lucky we were to be part of such a momentous occasion, surrounded by so much talent and inspiration.

As the week unfolded, I found myself cherishing the extraordinary memories we were creating. One of the highlights was covering the back media room of the Emmys for FENIX TV. There, I had the privilege felt like a reminder that we are all part of a larger tapestry, woven together by our shared love for storytelling and the arts.

Photo Credit: Tyme Journey

of interviewing stars from some of the most-watched television programs. Each conversation was a window into the passion and dedication that drives these remarkable individuals.

Witnessing history being made again was a life-changing experience. The excitement in the air was infectious as we celebrated not just the achievements of the nominees but the spirit of the industry itself. The camaraderie, the laughter, and the shared stories created a profound sense of belonging among everyone present.

This week wasn't just about the glitz and glamour; it was about the connections we forged and the inspiration we gained. In a world that often feels disconnected, Emmys Week reminded us of the power of community and the importance of uplifting one another. Each interaction

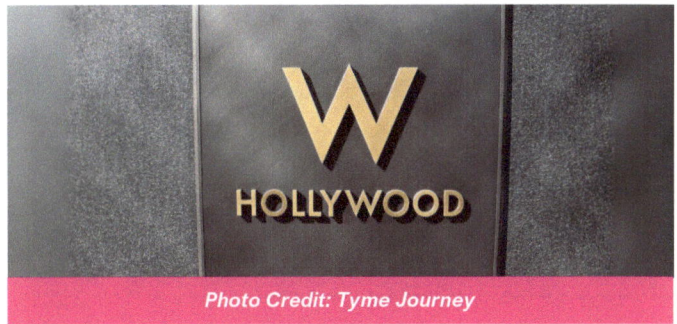

Photo Credit: Tyme Journey

As we packed up our memories and experiences to return home, I felt a renewed sense of purpose and motivation. This journey to Hollywood wasn't merely a trip; it was a profound reminder of the magic that happens when creativity and passion collide. I left with not only extraordinary memories but also a deep appreciation for the kindness and generosity that can be found in the heart of the entertainment industry.

Reflecting on our time at the Emmys Week, I realized that the true essence of Hollywood lies in its people—those who create, inspire, and connect. I am grateful for the opportunity to be a part of this incredible journey, and I look forward to carrying the spirit of that week into all my future endeavors. The excitement of that drive from Las Vegas to Hollywood will forever remain etched in my memory as a testament to the power of dreams and the magic that can unfold when we chase them.

CONNECT WITH US
www.fenixtv.app

UNLOCKING THE POWER OF WEALTHY MINDSET AND WELLNESS: A HOLISTIC APPROACH

by Lovely LaGuerre

Lovely LaGuerre, a powerhouse in the realms of real estate, entrepreneurship, and empowerment, brings her wisdom and experience to the forefront in her latest book, "The Wealthy Mindset and Wellness: A Holistic Approach." Through her own journey as a successful real estate agent and entrepreneur, Lovely has discovered the transformative power of adopting a holistic approach to health and well-being.

In today's world, there exists a profound disparity in both wealth and health. Lovely sheds light on this issue and offers a solution: a holistic approach that encompasses not only physical health but also mental and emotional well-being. By addressing the root causes of imbalance and prioritizing self-care, individuals can achieve greater overall wellness and prosperity.

At the heart of Lovely's message is the concept of a wealthy mindset—a mindset grounded in abundance, positivity, and self-worth. This mindset is essential for attracting wealth and success into one's life and is a cornerstone of holistic living. By adopting a wealthy mindset, individuals can break free from limiting beliefs and achieve their fullest potential.

But a wealthy mindset is just one piece of the puzzle. Lovely emphasizes the importance of taking a holistic approach to health and wellness, which includes practices such as meditation, intuitive eating, and regular physical activity. These practices not only promote physical health but also support mental and emotional well-being, creating a more balanced and fulfilling life.

One of the key takeaways from Lovely's book is the idea that health is wealth. By prioritizing self-care and adopting healthy lifestyle habits, individuals can create a foundation for success in all areas of life. Whether it's getting enough sleep, practicing mindfulness, or staying active, every small step towards better health contributes to overall well-being.

Lovely also addresses the importance of addressing the root causes of health issues rather than just treating the symptoms. By taking a holistic approach to health, individuals can uncover underlying issues and make meaningful changes that lead to long-term wellness.

"The Wealthy Mindset and Wellness: A Holistic Approach" offers readers a roadmap to greater health, happiness, and prosperity. Through her insightful guidance and practical advice, Lovely LaGuerre empowers readers to take control of their health and well-being and unlock their fullest potential. Whether you're a woman, an entrepreneur, or anyone looking to improve your life, this book is a valuable resource for creating lasting change.

CONNECT WITH LOVELY

IG: @PureHeavenlyHair
IG: @LovelyVegasCommercialLV
https://instagram.com/pureheavenlyhair
www.facebook.com/pureheavenlyhairboutique
www.PureHeavenlyHair.com
www.LovelyInspireYou.com
www.LovelySellsVegas.com

PRIYA ALI: HARNESSING THE POWER OF ENERGI FOR HOLISTIC WELLNESS

Priya Ali's journey from a young empathetic child to a seasoned intuitive healer is nothing short of remarkable. In her chapter "Everything Is Energi," she unveils the transformative power of energy in shaping our physical, emotional, and spiritual well-being.

From an early age, Priya possessed a unique gift: the ability to perceive the energy fields surrounding individuals. This innate sensitivity laid the foundation for her eventual career as an empath, intuitive, and healer. Yet, it wasn't until her 20s that she fully embraced her intuitive talents and began using them to facilitate healing and transformation in others.

Priya's initial foray into healing was marked by a sense of frustration. Despite achieving positive results with her clients, she found that their issues often resurfaced after a few months, leading her to question the permanence of her interventions. It was through deep introspection and meditation that she gained a profound insight: true healing requires a holistic approach that addresses the interconnectedness of mind, body, and spirit.

Armed with this newfound understanding, Priya embarked on a journey to integrate physical and energetic healing modalities. Teaming up with a functional medicine doctor, she developed a comprehensive approach that combined energetic healing with conventional medical treatments. The results were promising, yet Priya still sensed a missing piece of the puzzle.

It was through meditation and reflection that Priya uncovered the key to lasting transformation: alignment of mind, body, and spirit. Recognizing that each element of our being operates from its own unique energy, she devised a customized approach to healing that addressed the vibrational harmony of the entire being.

Central to Priya's philosophy is the understanding that everything is energy. Just as our physical bodies are composed of atoms and molecules, our thoughts, emotions, and actions emit energetic vibrations that impact our well-being. By cultivating awareness of these energies and aligning them with our intentions, we can facilitate profound healing and transformation.

Priya's holistic approach to wellness has yielded remarkable results, ranging from physical ailments to emotional traumas. Through her guidance, clients have experienced reversals of paralysis, restoration of eyesight, shrinkage of tumors, and recovery from eating disorders, addictions, anxiety, and depression.

Yet, Priya's ultimate goal extends beyond individual healing to empower others to become their own healers. By tapping into their innate intuitive abilities and cultivating awareness of their mind-body-spirit connection, individuals can advocate for their well-being and live a life of heightened awareness and vitality.

In essence, Priya's work underscores the profound truth that everything is energy. By embracing this fundamental principle and harnessing the power of energi for holistic wellness, we can unlock the full potential of our being and embark on a journey of profound healing and transformation.

CONNECT WITH PRIYA

www.linkedin.com/in/priya-ali-3237487
www.instagram.com/startliving365
www.facebook.com/priya.ali
www.living365wellness.love
www.energi.love

NICOLE CURTIS: A GUIDE FOR MOMS SUPPORTING STRUGGLING TEENS

Nicole Curtis, a passionate speaker, author, and mentor, is dedicated to empowering women to grow, elevate, and succeed in life and business. With a heart for supporting mothers with struggling teens, Nicole's mission is to provide valuable resources and authentic connections to women around the world. As a mental health advocate, Nicole offers guidance and encouragement to moms navigating the challenges of supporting their teen's mental well-being.

In her chapter, "A Mental Health 'Check-In' List for Moms With Struggling Teens," Nicole shares her personal journey as the mother of a teen girl battling major depression and anxiety. Through years of hospitalizations, counseling sessions, and sleepless nights, Nicole has gained valuable insights into the importance of protecting one's own mental health while supporting a struggling teen.

Nicole acknowledges the universal experience of mothers feeling a deep sense of heartache for their children's suffering. She emphasizes the need for moms to prioritize their own mental well-being, even amidst the chaos and challenges of supporting a struggling teen.

The chapter offers a practical "Mental Health 'Check-In' List" for moms, designed to help them navigate the emotional rollercoaster of supporting a teen's mental health journey. Nicole encourages moms to embrace their emotions and give themselves permission to feel, even when it's painful or overwhelming.

Through journaling and self-reflection, Nicole highlights the importance of processing emotions and seeking support from other moms who understand the journey. She emphasizes the need for moms to recognize their own limitations and avoid internalizing their teen's struggles as a reflection of their parenting abilities.

One of the key lessons Nicole shares is the realization that moms can't *"fix"* their teen's mental health struggles. Despite their best efforts, moms may feel helpless and frustrated when their support is rejected or met with resistance. Nicole encourages moms to focus on supporting their teen's journey while maintaining boundaries and self-care practices.

Nicole also addresses common challenges faced by moms, such as navigating communication with their struggling teen and overcoming the fear of triggering negative reactions. She shares her own struggles with walking on eggshells and offers practical strategies for setting boundaries and maintaining parental authority while still showing love and support.

Ultimately, Nicole's chapter is a heartfelt message of solidarity and support for moms navigating the complex terrain of supporting a struggling teen's mental health. Through vulnerability and honesty, Nicole reminds moms that they are not alone in their journey and that self-care is essential for providing the best support to their teens.

As Nicole dedicates her chapter to all the courageous moms supporting struggling teens, she extends her love and encouragement to those who may be facing similar challenges. With her guidance and compassion, Nicole Curtis offers a beacon of hope for moms navigating the often tumultuous waters of teen mental health.

CONNECT WITH NICOLE

www.linkedin.com/in/nicole-curtis-sherisesstudios
www.facebook.com/nicolecurtiscrazychickenlady
www.instagram.com/nicolecurtiscrazychickenlady
www.sherisesstudios.com
www.facebook.com/groups/sherisesstudioscommunity

MINH VU: A JOURNEY OF HOLISTIC HEALING AND MIRACLES

Minh Vu, CEO, and founder of Endotransformation, has emerged as a beacon of hope and inspiration for women battling endometriosis and infertility. Through her own firsthand experience with stage 4 endometriosis and infertility, Minh has not only overcome immense challenges but has also defied the odds by naturally conceiving twin boys. Her journey from pain and despair to healing and joy serves as a testament to the power of holistic health and the resilience of the human spirit.

In her chapter, "Light & The Protective Warrior," Minh shares poignant lessons learned from her journey, each narrated from a unique perspective that captures the depth of her experiences.

Lesson #1: Be Your Own Health Advocate
Minh's journey began with three years of unsuccessful attempts to conceive, culminating in a diagnosis of stage 4 endometriosis. Devastated by the news of infertility, Minh embarked on a quest to reclaim her health and fertility through holistic means. With unwavering determination, she committed to being her own health advocate, embracing a holistic lifestyle that ultimately restored balance to her body and alleviated her chronic pain. Through this transformative journey, Minh discovered the power of self-advocacy and the importance of trusting her intuition in navigating her health challenges.

Lesson #2: God Still Performs Miracles
Amidst the turmoil of infertility and endometriosis, Minh and her husband Tom experienced the miraculous joy of conceiving twin boys. Their journey, however, was fraught with challenges, including complications such as Twin-to-Twin Transfusion Syndrome (TTTS) and placental abruption. Through moments of fear and uncertainty, Minh and Tom remained steadfast in their faith, believing in the possibility of miracles. Their sons, Luke and Liam, became symbols of resilience and hope, embodying the transformative power of love and faith in the face of adversity.

Lesson #3: Keep the Faith
Throughout her journey, Minh confronted fears of inadequacy, rejection, and hopelessness, ultimately finding solace in faith and self-discovery. Embracing her inner strength and resilience, Minh learned to overcome obstacles with grace and determination. Her message of hope and empowerment resonates deeply with women battling similar challenges, offering a beacon of light in the darkest of times.

Minh's journey serves as a powerful reminder that healing is possible, even in the face of seemingly insurmountable obstacles. Through her work at Endotransformation, Minh continues to empower women to advocate for their own health and embrace holistic healing. Her message of resilience, faith, and empowerment inspires countless individuals to embrace their own journeys of healing and transformation.

MICHELE KLINE: REDISCOVERING LIFE'S SYMPHONY

In the hustle and bustle of modern life, it's easy to lose sight of the simple joys that surround us. For Michele Kline, a seasoned leader in the Hospitality Industry, the wake-up call came in the form of birds chirping—a moment of clarity that sparked a journey of self-discovery and transformation.

In her chapter, "I Hear Birds Chirping," Michele candidly shares her experience of burnout—a state of emotional, physical, and mental exhaustion that left her feeling depleted and disconnected from the world around her. Through introspection and self-reflection, Michele recognized the toll that her career-driven lifestyle had taken on her well-being, prompting her to reevaluate her priorities and reclaim her sense of purpose.

Drawing from her own journey of healing and growth, Michele offers a series of actionable insights and practical tools for navigating life's challenges with grace and resilience. From embracing self-worth and setting boundaries to prioritizing rest and authenticity, Michele's wisdom serves as a guiding light for those seeking to cultivate a life of meaning and fulfillment.

At the heart of Michele's message lies a profound truth: true leadership begins with self-awareness and self-care. By prioritizing her own well-being and listening to the whispers of her heart, Michele discovered a newfound sense of purpose and vitality—a transformation that has empowered her to lead with authenticity and compassion.

As a seasoned coach and mentor, Michele is committed to empowering others to unlock their full potential and live their best lives. Through her work with individuals and organizations, Michele shares her wealth of knowledge and expertise, inspiring others to embrace their inner ninja warrior and seize control of their destiny.

In a world filled with noise and distraction, Michele's story serves as a powerful reminder to pause, listen, and appreciate the beauty that surrounds us. By tuning into the symphony of life and embracing each moment with gratitude and awareness, we can find peace, purpose, and joy in the simplest of pleasures.

Michele Kline's journey is a testament to the power of resilience, self-discovery, and the transformative potential of intentional living. Through her courageous pursuit of authenticity and wholeness, Michele invites us all to embark on our own journey of self-discovery and rediscover the magic of life's symphony.

CONNECT WITH MICHELE

www.linkedin.com/in/michelekline
www.facebook.com/klinehospitalityconsulting
www.instagram.com/michelklinekhc
www.klinehospitality.com
www.klinehospitality.com/services

Why Should You Drink Water?

You have probably heard that water makes up over 70% of the body, right? Water is part of all body fluids and is vital to the proper function of the body's organ systems. It should be obvious then that the quality of the water you drink is extremely important. For your body to be at optimal health, you should drink only the purest and cleanest water possible.

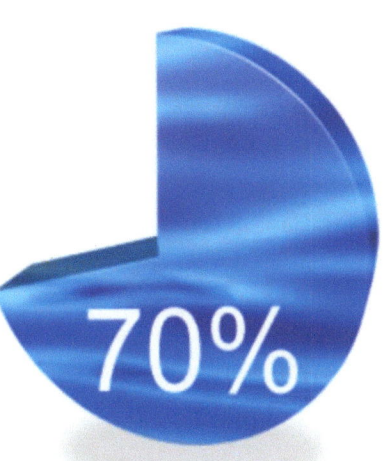

**For more information, email
MyDailyWaterforHealth@gmail.com**

Get your Kangen Water® System TODAY!

The Kangen Alkaline Ionized Water System is compact and easy to install in any home or office. It will conveniently transform your tap water into healthy, balanced water that is perfect for your lifestyle and your wellness goals.

MASTERING THE WELLNESS MINDSET: A GUIDE BY PAMELA KURT

In her enlightening chapter "Mindset is the key to wellness," Pamela Kurt, a distinguished attorney, business owner, and advocate for women's empowerment, delves into the transformative power of mindset in achieving holistic wellness. Drawing on her expertise in coaching and personal development, Kurt offers valuable insights and practical strategies for cultivating a wellness mindset and living a fulfilling life.

Kurt begins by emphasizing the foundational role of mindset in the pursuit of wellness. As Richard Davidson aptly said, "The key to a healthy life is having a healthy mind." Kurt asserts that true wellness starts from within, with a conscious decision to prioritize one's mental, emotional, and spiritual well-being.

Central to Kurt's philosophy is the notion that our thoughts shape our reality. She firmly believes that *"Your thoughts become things,"* emphasizing the profound impact of our mindset on our health and overall quality of life. By adopting a positive and proactive mindset, individuals can unlock their full potential and experience profound transformations in their well-being.

But what exactly is the wellness mindset? According to Kurt, it is an awareness of the importance of health and well-being, coupled with a commitment to nurturing oneself at a holistic level. It entails making self-care a priority and consistently pursuing a lifestyle that supports physical, emotional, and spiritual health.

In her chapter, Kurt offers a wealth of practical tips for cultivating a wellness mindset and prioritizing self-care. From getting adequate sleep and reducing stress to fostering healthy relationships and practicing gratitude, Kurt provides actionable strategies for nurturing one's overall well-being.

One of the key takeaways from Kurt's chapter is the importance of self-compassion and self-care. She emphasizes the need for individuals, especially women who often juggle multiple roles and responsibilities, to prioritize their own well-being and set boundaries to avoid burnout.

Kurt also highlights the significance of consistency in maintaining a wellness mindset. By making small, sustainable changes to daily habits and routines, individuals can gradually shift their mindset and experience lasting improvements in their health and happiness.

Throughout her chapter, Kurt's passion for empowering women to prioritize their well-being shines through. She encourages readers to embrace self-love, practice gratitude, and surround themselves with like-minded individuals who support their journey to wellness.

Kurt leaves readers with a powerful reminder: *"Feed the good wolf in your head, and wellness will prevail."* By adopting a wellness mindset and committing to self-care, individuals can unlock their full potential and live their best lives.

Whether you're just beginning your wellness journey or seeking to deepen your commitment to self-care, Pamela Kurt's insightful chapter offers invaluable guidance and inspiration. With her practical tips and empowering message, Kurt empowers readers to take charge of their health and well-being, one positive thought at a time.

CONNECT WITH PAMELA

www.instagram.com/best_version_you
www.facebook.com/bestversionyou
www.linkedin.com/in/pamela-kurt-41a26ba
www.BestVersionYou.com
www.PamKurt.com

UNLOCKING YOUR POTENTIAL: THE POWER OF UNDERSTANDING YOUR CYCLE

by Lauren Weiss

In the bustling landscape of modern life, women often find themselves navigating the ebb and flow of their hormonal cycles amidst a whirlwind of responsibilities and expectations. Yet, amidst the chaos, there lies a profound opportunity for women to harness the innate power of their monthly cycle and unlock a new realm of health, vitality, and well-being. Enter Lauren Weiss, a visionary leader in the realm of women's health and wellness, whose groundbreaking Cycle Align Method™ offers a transformative approach to embracing and leveraging the cyclical nature of the female body.

With a lifelong history of hormonal and menstrual cycle challenges, Lauren embarked on a personal quest to decode the intricate nuances of her own body, cycle, and feminine essence. Armed with a deep reservoir of research and self-awareness, she unearthed a profound revelation: the key to women's health and empowerment lies in understanding and honoring the natural rhythms of their bodies.

In her enlightening chapter, "Mind Your Flow," Lauren invites women on a journey to explore the dynamic interplay between their menstrual cycle and brain function. Drawing upon compelling scientific research, she illuminates the profound impact of hormonal fluctuations on cognitive function and emotional well-being across the menstrual cycle.

During the Menstrual Phase, characterized by a dip in hormone levels, women may experience fluctuations in mood, memory, and emotional regulation. Armed with this awareness, Lauren advocates for self-compassion and gentle self-care practices to navigate this phase with grace and ease.

As the cycle progresses into the Follicular Phase, marked by a surge in estrogen levels, women may find themselves infused with energy and creativity. Lauren encourages women to embrace this surge of vitality by engaging in creative pursuits and social activities that nourish the soul and ignite the spirit of exploration.

During Ovulation, when estrogen levels peak, women experience heightened social acuity and emotional resonance. Lauren advocates for embracing this phase as an opportunity for connection, communication, and community engagement.

Finally, as the cycle transitions into the Luteal Phase, characterized by elevated progesterone levels, women may experience shifts in mood and cognitive function. Lauren emphasizes the importance of self-soothing practices and stress management techniques to navigate this phase with serenity and balance.

Through her insightful exploration of the menstrual cycle's influence on brain function and emotional well-being, Lauren empowers women to embrace their cyclical nature and cultivate a deeper connection with their bodies. By honoring the unique needs of each menstrual phase, women can optimize their mental health, enhance their overall well-being, and unlock their full potential.

In a world that often overlooks the profound wisdom encoded within the female body, Lauren Weiss stands as a guiding light—a champion of women's health and empowerment. With her revolutionary Cycle Align

Method™, she offers women a transformative pathway to embrace their feminine genius, thrive in every aspect of their lives, and unlock the boundless potential that resides within.

CONNECT WITH LAUREN

www.linkedin.com/in/lauren-e-weiss-female-cycle-advocate-00537a41
www.instagram.com/cyclealign
www.facebook.com/profile.php?id=100046109392085
www.cycleaglign.com
www.cyclealignme.com

LIFESTYLE &
Wellness

PEMF THERAPY:
A NATURAL PATH TO RECOVERY AND WELLNESS

by Andy Smith

In today's fast-paced world, where stress, discomfort, and fatigue have become constant companions, many are seeking holistic practices to restore balance and well-being. One practice gaining attention is Pulsed Electromagnetic Field (PEMF) therapy. This innovative therapy supports the body's natural recovery processes and promotes overall wellness without invasive treatments.

PEMF therapy works by delivering electromagnetic pulses that stimulate cellular activity. These gentle waves penetrate deep into the body, helping cells recharge and function more efficiently. By improving circulation, reducing inflammation, and promoting restful sleep, PEMF offers a comprehensive, holistic approach to health. It's an ideal solution for anyone looking to optimise their well-being naturally.

Physical Benefits of PEMF Therapy:
- **Pain Relief**: PEMF is commonly used to manage pain by reducing inflammation and promoting faster recovery from injuries or chronic conditions such as arthritis.
- **Improved Circulation**: By boosting blood flow, PEMF helps the body deliver oxygen and nutrients to tissues more efficiently, supporting healing and recovery.
- **Faster Recovery from Injuries**: PEMF stimulates the body's repair mechanisms, helping to speed up recovery from sprains, strains, and even bone fractures.
- **Enhanced Physical Vitality**: Whether used as part of a recovery plan or as a preventive measure, PEMF supports overall physical energy and vitality by improving cellular function.

Mental and Emotional Benefits of PEMF Therapy:
- **Stress Reduction**: PEMF helps to regulate the nervous system, promoting relaxation and reducing stress levels, making it an excellent complement to mindfulness practices like yoga and meditation.
- **Better Sleep Quality**: By supporting deep, restful sleep, PEMF therapy helps the body rejuvenate overnight, leaving you refreshed and energized.
- **Enhanced Cognitive Function**: By improving circulation and oxygenation, PEMF therapy can help boost mental clarity, focus, and cognitive performance.

As awareness grows about the importance of maintaining cellular health, PEMF therapy has found its place in wellness centres, homes, and even the recovery routines of professional athletes. With its ability to reduce pain, enhance sleep quality, and accelerate recovery, PEMF seamlessly complements other self-care practices such as yoga, meditation, and proper nutrition.

The **CELLER8** device is a cutting-edge addition to the PEMF market, backed by over a decade of expertise in the field. It's designed with the modern user in mind, offering a 2-in-1 solution for both localized and full-body sessions. Not only is it portable and user-friendly, but it also delivers impressive intensities tailored to suit a range of therapeutic needs. Whether you're looking to address specific areas of discomfort or boost overall vitality, the CELLER8 makes incorporating PEMF therapy into your routine easier than ever.

Andy Smith is a wellness advocate and Founder of CELLER8 and NewMed Ltd, a company specialising in Pulsed Electromagnetic Field (PEMF) therapy devices. During a challenging period following a health scare, NewMed founder Andy discovered the power of Pulsed Electromagnetic Field (PEMF) therapy. After experiencing severe stomach pain that led to emergency surgery, traditional treatments and antibiotics failed to resolve his infection. Remembering a PEMF device used for his father's horses, Andy tried it for himself, and within a week, his pain disappeared, and the infection healed. Motivated by his remarkable recovery, Andy founded NewMed Ltd and created CELLER8 to make PEMF therapy more accessible in the UK, helping others benefit from the same transformative technology.

CONNECT WITH ANDY

Instagram: @celler8
Facebook: @celler8
LinkedIn: @celler8

KIM RENDON: EMPOWERING WOMEN THROUGH MENOPAUSE EDUCATION

Kim Rendon, a registered dietitian and certified lactation specialist with over 30 years of experience, is on a mission to destigmatize and educate women about perimenopause and menopause. As the founder of her own integrative health coaching business, Kim brings a wealth of knowledge and passion to her advocacy for women's health.

In her chapter, "Become an Ageless Goddess," Kim shares her personal journey through perimenopause and menopause, offering insights and practical advice for women navigating this transformative stage of life.

Perimenopause, often described as puberty in reverse, can be a tumultuous time characterized by hormonal fluctuations and a myriad of symptoms. Kim candidly recounts her experience of going through perimenopause while raising teenage boys, juggling multiple responsibilities, and grappling with overwhelming exhaustion and depression. Her story resonates with countless women who silently struggle with the physical and emotional challenges of perimenopause.

Through her own journey of self-discovery and research, Kim realized the importance of normalizing discussions around menopause and empowering women to take control of their health. Menopause, she emphasizes, is not just about hot flashes and mood swings—it encompasses a wide range of symptoms that can significantly impact a woman's quality of life.

Kim sheds light on the often-overlooked symptoms of perimenopause, from heart palpitations and joint pain to digestive issues and memory challenges. By raising awareness of these symptoms, Kim aims to empower women to recognize and address the hormonal imbalances that may be contributing to their discomfort.

Central to Kim's approach is the recognition of the interconnectedness between diet, lifestyle, and hormonal health. She emphasizes the importance of nourishing the body with whole, nutrient-dense foods, eliminating processed foods and sugar, and prioritizing gut health through probiotics and toxin reduction.

In addition to dietary recommendations, Kim advocates for lifestyle changes that can support hormonal balance and overall well-being. From stress reduction techniques like meditation and journaling to prioritizing sleep and addressing past traumas, Kim offers practical strategies for women to optimize their health during perimenopause and beyond.

Kim's own health journey serves as a testament to the transformative power of holistic self-care. By making small, sustainable changes to her diet and lifestyle, Kim has experienced increased energy, mental clarity, and weight loss without sacrificing her well-being.

As women embark on their own menopause journeys, Kim encourages them to embrace this stage of life as an opportunity for growth and self-discovery. Rather than viewing menopause as the beginning of the end, Kim invites women to become ageless goddesses—embracing their inner strength, wisdom, and beauty.

Through her work and advocacy, Kim Rendon is empowering women to navigate perimenopause and menopause with confidence, resilience, and grace. By fostering open conversations and providing practical support, Kim is helping women reclaim their health, vitality, and sense of self during this transformative stage of life.

CONNECT WITH KIM

www.linkedin.com/in/kim-rendon-824073218
www.facebook.com/kimcoaches2020
www.instagram.com/livethrive_wellness
www.livethrivewellness.com

THRIVING BEYOND CHRONIC ILLNESS: MY JOURNEY OF HEALING THROUGH HEALTHY HABITS AND MINDSET SHIFTS

by Sonya McDonald, RN, BSN, BCC

For over 16 years, I have lived with Rheumatoid Arthritis (RA) and Fibromyalgia, conditions that can be both physically and emotionally challenging. However, instead of allowing these chronic illnesses to define me, I chose to embark on a journey of transformation—a journey that has allowed me to manage my symptoms and thrive. As a Board-Certified Transformational Life Coach and Registered Nurse, I now dedicate my life to helping others do the same.

When I was first diagnosed, I felt overwhelmed and unsure of how to manage my health. Like many, I initially relied only on medication to handle the pain and inflammation that came with RA and Fibromyalgia. While medication was essential, I knew there had to be more I could do. I began exploring alternative ways to manage my symptoms, leading me to adopt healthy habits, mindset shifts, and dietary changes that have since transformed my life.

THE POWER OF HEALTHY HABITS
One of the first changes I made was incorporating daily habits that promote physical and mental well-being. Walking in nature became a cornerstone of my routine. Not only did it keep my body moving, but it also brought clarity, inspiration, and peace. Walking became a form of meditation, helping me reduce stress and promote a positive mindset.

I also began journaling my gratitude's daily. This simple habit helped me focus on the positive aspects of my life. By consistently practicing gratitude, I found my stress levels decreased, which helped reduce inflammation in my body.

DIETARY CHANGES AND THE IMPACT OF CELERY JUICE
Diet played a significant role in my journey to better health. I reduced inflammatory foods like processed sugars and refined carbs from my diet, focusing instead on whole, nutrient-dense foods. This dietary shift had a profound impact on my energy and well-being. One of the most transformative changes I made was incorporating celery juice into my daily routine. Known for its anti-inflammatory properties, celery juice helped reduce inflammation in my body. Over time, I noticed a significant improvement in my symptoms, including less pain and stiffness, which allowed me to engage in activities I had once thought impossible.

MINDSET SHIFTS: CHOOSING TO THRIVE
While physical habits and dietary changes were crucial, the most profound transformation came from shifting my mindset. Instead of viewing myself as a victim of chronic illness, I chose to see myself as someone who could thrive despite it.

This mindset shift was empowering. It allowed me to take ownership of my health, be proactive in managing my symptoms, and embrace the journey of personal growth. I learned to listen to my body and prioritize self-care. Letting go of the need to be perfect, I focused on being the best version of myself.

HELPING OTHERS ON THEIR JOURNEY
As a Board-Certified Transformational Life Coach and Registered Nurse, I now help others navigate their journey to wellness. I believe no one should be defined by their chronic illness. With the right mindset, habits, and support, it's possible to live a full, vibrant life and thrive.

If you are living with chronic illness, know that you are not alone. There is hope, and there are ways to manage symptoms, reduce inflammation, and live well. By adopting healthy habits, making dietary changes, and shifting your mindset, you can take control of your health and your life. You have the power to be the best version of yourself—let me help you on your journey to wellness and beyond.

CONNECT WITH SONYA

www.sonyamcdonald.com
www.smcdonald25.myrandf.com
www.instagram.com/sonyamcdonald
www.facebook.com/sonya.mcdonald.96
www.linkedin.com/in/sonya-mcdonald-rn-bsn-bcc-7786521b9

UNLOCKING THE POWER OF HORMONES: THE SHE EATS METHOD BY KATIE MARKEL

In her chapter "Surviving to Thriving," Katie Markel, CEO of She Eats, delivers a refreshing take on women's health and nutrition. Markel's journey from traditional dieting to hormone syncing is a testament to the transformative power of understanding one's body.

Markel begins by acknowledging the common struggles faced by women in their quest for health and weight management. From restrictive diets to relentless exercise routines, many women find themselves trapped in a cycle of frustration and disappointment. Markel challenges this narrative by introducing the concept of hormone syncing—a method that works with the body's natural rhythms rather than against them.

At the heart of Markel's approach is the recognition that women's hormones play a pivotal role in metabolism, energy levels, and overall well-being. By aligning nutrition and fitness with the fluctuations of the menstrual cycle, women can optimize their health and say goodbye to common symptoms like PMS, low energy, and mood swings.

One of the key insights Markel shares is the importance of understanding the four phases of the menstrual cycle and how they impact dietary needs. From carb-friendly days to fat-burning phases, Markel provides practical guidance on tailoring nutrition to support hormonal balance and maximize results.

Central to the She Eats Method is the concept of cycle syncing—a personalized approach to nutrition and fitness that empowers women to work with their bodies rather than against them. By tracking their menstrual cycles and adjusting their dietary choices accordingly, women can achieve sustainable weight management and vibrant health.

Markel's chapter is not just about weight loss or physical performance; it's about reclaiming control over one's health and well-being. Through hormone syncing, women can experience newfound energy, confidence, and freedom from restrictive dieting practices.

The She Eats Method isn't just a diet—it's a lifestyle. By adopting this holistic approach to health and nutrition, women can transform their relationship with food and fitness, paving the way for a happier, healthier future.

Markel's message is clear: every woman deserves to feel her best. Through the She Eats Community, she's on a mission to empower women to take charge of their health and embrace a lifestyle that nourishes body, mind, and soul.

For those ready to embark on their own journey to health and happiness, Markel offers a free framework for implementing the She Eats Method. With access to valuable resources and a supportive community, women can start thriving today.

From Sound Waves to Brainwaves: Discover INSTANT ZEN

Charel's life took an unexpected turn when an injury paused her Hollywood career, leading her to heal her ankle with scalar wave technology—an early glimpse into the quantum healing she had been exploring. Combining quantum principles, shamanic wisdom, and the power of words, she laid the foundation for her future healing work.

A chance encounter with a healer who blended the teachings of Jesus with a 4,000-year-old Buddhist lineage further enriched her journey. From this fusion of sound engineering, quantum healing, and spiritual balance, INSTANT ZEN was born.

INSTANT ZEN Offers You

Boost Creativity & Problem-Solving: Just as Charel fine-tuned sound waves, she'll help fine-tune your thoughts using quantum principles. Transform your mind from chaotic to harmonious.

- Enhance Emotional Intelligence: Learn to read emotional energies like a shaman while maintaining mindful awareness. Improve relationships with clarity and compassion.
- Prevent Burnout: Discover the work-life balance Charel mastered by blending ancient wisdom with modern science. Make your career a source of energy, not stress.
- The cornerstone of INSTANT ZEN? The revolutionary "60-Second Zen Zaps" – quick, powerful techniques rooted in quantum healing and mindfulness that bring you from frazzled to focused faster than you can say "Om!"

At the heart of INSTANT ZEN are the "60-Second Zen Zaps"—quick, powerful techniques rooted in quantum healing and mindfulness to bring you from stressed to centered in just a moment.

Choose Your Zen Path:

Join our group sessions for collective growth
Opt for one-on-one coaching for personalized transformation
Attention Business Owners: Is stress creating static in your team's performance?
Let INSTANT ZEN clear the airways to success with its unique blend of ancient wisdom and modern science.

Ready to take the leap from "Oh no!" to "Om"?

SHE GLOWS:
WHEN HER CUP RUNNETH OVER

by Carmen K. Maendel

MY IDENTITY IN CHRIST

Hello friend, I am Carmen K. Maendel and I am a child of God. I rededicated my life to Christ on November 04, 2006 after coming to the Lord at the young age of thirteen. God has worked in amazing ways in the areas of fitness and nutrition and overall wellness and self-care in both my personal and professional life. I have an immense passion for this topic and devoted eight years of my life training more than fifty women in our Maendel Fitness Gym. In my chapter, When Her Cup Runneth Over for the book: She Glows, I share real life examples of how God has worked in my life and provide resources to you, for your convenience, to aid in your own wellness and self-care journey.

MY STORY: FROM DIM TO RADIANT

A woman glows when she is loved, cared for, appreciated, feels useful to others, and is working in an area she is deeply passionate about. All women are beautiful regardless of their size, body type, or bone structure. Confidence is feeling amazing with the body God blessed you with, and respecting your body as the temple of Holy Spirit. Confidence is your identity in Christ and not a number on the scale. It's all about rockin' what you got! I share my story about a time that I was not as confident as the woman I am today, and some of the adversity and challenges that have come up during my life. I share how I moved from dim to radiant, and how God worked in specific areas of my life to help me build that confidence and assurance in myself, but even more importantly who I was in Christ.

MAENDEL FITNESS: FOUNDING THE COMPANY
2016 - 2023

I started viewing diet and exercise as a lifestyle, and I got into the best shape of my life. In my chapter, I specifically outline secret strategies and simple things you can do to achieve a higher level of fitness, and major health and wellness transformation in your own life. I have been able to maintain this level of fitness well into my early 50's. I talk about how many days you need to do something to create a habit, and I share major breakthroughs that I had working with my clients following God's guidance and direction. I share about educating my clients about health, fitness, and using proper form and techniques to maximize weight loss and ultimate health and fitness goals.

I talk about my own story and how I used SMART goals and repetition for myself and my clients to achieve incredible results. I liked to *"teach my clients to fish"* instead of *"giving them fish."* This means that they

graduated from my program being able to create their own workouts in any gym, use correct form and exercise technique, and able to navigate along in their own fitness journey without me, their fitness trainer. I talk about the importance of the 80/20 philosophy and how that relates to diet and exercise in my chapter: When Her Cup Runneth Over. I pushed my clients to their limits, however I do understand that everyone has a limited capacity they can reach. I was sensitive to that and always tried to set my clients up for success, not failure. I had a specific rule for myself that I would never ask my clients to do something that I would not be able and willing to do myself. Often times I trained my clients by leading by example. There are lots of useful tips and tricks, golden nuggets of health and fitness advice and guidance in this chapter, culminated through years of practice and small to large victories in the various disciplines.

END OF THE CHAPTER FITNESS & NUTRITION RESOURCES

I include a list of Biblical Affirmations with scripture references to help encourage and give you a solid foundation to grow from. At the end of the chapter, I include various fitness and nutrition resources with links to access the information with Google drive. I included my YouTube channel link which I created several videos about health and nutrition, and lots of fitness videos that you can do with me as well. I include the MFC Muscle Menu link that will be helpful to you to create your own workouts, and MFC Guru Grocery List which will help you shop for healthy foods and know what vitamins and minerals are in each food. I even include a link for the MFC Tasty & Savory Cookbook with healthy delicious recipes you can make and serve in your own home. The last two links are the MFC Confidence Boost System and the MFC I Can Statements. Wonderful resources to help boost confidence and feel better about yourself.

My hope and prayer is that you will use these resources to help you with your own personal wellness and self-care journey. I hope this chapter and these health and fitness resources are a tremendous blessing to all of you. Wishing you all the very best in your own individual wellness and self-care journey!

Photo Credit: Heidi Adele Photography

CONNECT WITH CARMEN

www.natespropertymaintenance.com
www.facebook.com/ncmaendel
www.facebook.com/profile.php?id=100093303554586
www.instagram.com/maendelcarmen

NAVIGATING FINANCIAL WELLNESS WITH HEATHER STOKES BENTON

In her illuminating chapter "Wealth Health," Heather Stokes Benton, a dedicated wife, mother, homeschooler, and business owner, sheds light on the profound interplay between financial well-being and mental health. Drawing on her personal experiences and professional insights, Benton offers invaluable guidance and practical strategies for achieving financial wellness and unlocking greater peace of mind.

Benton begins by highlighting the undeniable correlation between financial worries and mental health challenges such as depression, anxiety, and substance abuse. Citing research published in the esteemed medical journal JAMA Psychiatry, Benton underscores the detrimental impact of low household income on mental wellness, emphasizing the need for proactive measures to address financial stressors.

Recognizing the significance of money in shaping our lives, Benton acknowledges the pervasive negative attitudes and beliefs surrounding finances. From generational trauma to historical standards and gender inequality, Benton delves into the complex factors that influence our relationship with money, urging readers to challenge and redefine their perspectives.

Central to Benton's approach is the concept of financial trauma—an often overlooked aspect of mental health discourse. By acknowledging the intense emotions and psychological effects of financial struggles, Benton encourages individuals to confront and heal from past traumas, paving the way for greater financial stability and well-being.

In her chapter, Benton outlines a nine-step cure to money management, offering practical tips for organizing finances, tracking spending, and setting achievable goals. From living frugally and cutting unnecessary expenses to embracing intentional spending habits, Benton empowers readers to take control of their financial future.

Throughout her chapter, Benton's passion for helping families overcome financial challenges and build generational wealth shines through. Drawing on her own experiences of resilience and perseverance, Benton inspires readers to rewrite their financial path and embark on a journey from surviving to thriving.

Benton leaves readers with a powerful reminder: financial wellness is achievable. While it may require intentional actions and perseverance, Benton's chapter serves as a beacon of hope for individuals seeking to transform their relationship with money and secure a brighter future for themselves and their families.

Whether you're grappling with financial stressors or striving to cultivate a healthier mindset around money, Heather Stokes Benton's insightful chapter offers invaluable guidance and inspiration. With her compassionate approach and actionable advice, Benton empowers readers to embark on a journey toward financial wellness and greater peace of mind.

LIFE INSURANCE AWARENESS MONTH

DIVYA CHANDEGRA: NAVIGATING BALANCE AND SELF-LOVE

Divya Chandegra, a devoted life and wellness soul guide, embarks on a mission to empower parents and professionals to break free from limiting childhood beliefs and subconscious blocks. With a focus on inner child healing, generational patterns, and mindset reprogramming, Divya leads individuals on a transformative journey toward self-love and unconditional acceptance.

In her enlightening chapter, "Attract Fulfilment and Success Through Balance and Self-Love," Divya shares her personal evolution from a seasoned over-giver to a beacon of balance and self-awareness. Raised in a family where giving was synonymous with love, Divya recognized the detrimental impact of neglecting her own needs in favor of serving others.

Boundaries and Balance:
Divya candidly reflects on her struggle with setting healthy boundaries and finding balance in her life. Overcommitting to obligations and prioritizing the needs of others left her feeling drained and unfulfilled. Through introspection, she discovered the importance of prioritizing self-care and reclaiming her autonomy.

Wellness and Self-Care:
Drawing inspiration from Eartha Kitt's wisdom, Divya emphasizes the significance of falling in love with oneself as a foundation for genuine connection and fulfillment. She reflects on her journey of seeking external validation and the realization that true happiness stems from within.

The Impact of Our Childhood:
Divya delves into the impact of childhood conditioning on her ability to express herself authentically and identify her own needs. Through introspection and self-reflection, she unraveled deep-seated beliefs and embraced vulnerability as a catalyst for growth.

Connection With Others:
By fostering a deeper connection with herself, Divya transformed her relationships with others. She explores the importance of creating safe spaces for authentic communication and dismantling societal expectations that perpetuate conditional love.

Success and Self-Growth:
Divya redefines success as an ongoing journey of self-discovery and personal growth. By shedding limiting beliefs and embracing her true essence, she found fulfillment in living authentically and serving her purpose.

Creating the Life You Desire:
With a message of empowerment, Divya encourages readers to embrace their inner truth and chart their own path to fulfillment. Through conscious living and self-awareness, she believes individuals can manifest their desired reality and inspire positive change in the world.

As Divya continues her mission to guide others toward balance and self-love, she offers valuable resources, including her eBook "Success Starts with Self," designed to support individuals on their journey of personal transformation. Through her teachings, Divya invites individuals to embrace self-love as a catalyst for lasting fulfillment and success.

CONNECT WITH DIVYA

www.instagram.com/divya.chandegra
www.facebook.com/Life-and-Wellness-with-Divya-115873590689176
www.divya-chandegra.com
www.divya-chandegra.com/subscribe

ELEVATE

HANNA OLIVAS: EMPOWERING WOMEN THROUGH PERSONAL HEALTH JOURNEYS

Hanna Olivas, an influential author and speaker, has dedicated her life to empowering women to prioritize their health and wellness. As the founder of the Brave & Beautiful Blood Cancer Foundation and co-founder of She Rises Studios, Hanna's journey from a cancer diagnosis to becoming a leading advocate for women's health is both inspiring and impactful.

In her chapter, "The Journey is Personal," Hanna addresses the urgent need for women to prioritize their mental and physical well-being in the face of chronic diseases and other health challenges. With empathy and insight, she encourages readers to take control of their health and make positive changes for a better future.

Taking Control:
Hanna emphasizes the importance of taking control of one's mental and physical health, especially in the face of daunting health challenges like chronic diseases and cancer. By prioritizing self-care and healthy habits, women can proactively manage their well-being and improve their quality of life.

Breaking Routine:
She highlights the tendency for women to become trapped in unhealthy routines, such as sacrificing sleep for work or relying on fast food due to time constraints. Hanna urges readers to break free from these harmful patterns and make conscious choices that prioritize their health and happiness.

Overcoming Barriers:
Hanna acknowledges the barriers that women face in seeking help and support for their health issues. From societal expectations to personal reluctance, many women suffer in silence rather than reaching out for assistance. She encourages readers to overcome these barriers and seek the support they need to thrive.

Inspiring Stories:
Within the pages of the book, readers will find inspiring stories of women who have overcome significant health challenges. These stories serve as a source of motivation and encouragement for readers to embark on their own journey to optimal health and wellness.

Empowering Change:
Hanna empowers readers to embrace their journey towards becoming unstoppable women in health and wellness. By harnessing their inner strength and determination, women can take charge of their health and transform their lives for the better.

The Time is Now:
With a sense of urgency, Hanna reminds readers that the time to prioritize their health is now. Delaying self-care or ignoring warning signs can have serious consequences. She urges women to seize the opportunity to prioritize their well-being and start their journey towards a healthier, happier life.

As Hanna continues to advocate for women's health and wellness, she invites readers to join her in embracing personal empowerment and embracing their journey to becoming unstoppable women in health and wellness. Through education, support, and action, women can take control of their health and lead fulfilling lives.

CONNECT WITH HANNA

www.facebook.com/sherisesstudios
www.SheRisesStudios.com

THE CANDIDA DIET: WHAT TO EAT AND WHAT TO AVOID FOR LASTING RESULTS

by Dan Jackowiak

Candida is a type of yeast that naturally lives in places like your mouth, gut, and skin, usually without causing any problems. However, when the balance in your body is thrown off, whether due to a weakened immune system, dietary changes, or medications, Candida can start to grow uncontrollably; this overgrowth can lead to various symptoms, like digestive issues (bloating, constipation, diarrhea), recurrent yeast infections, skin rashes, oral thrush, brain fog, mood swings, joint pain, and sugar or carb cravings.

The Candida diet is designed to manage this overgrowth by cutting out foods that help Candida thrive, particularly sugar and refined carbs, and boosting foods that support your beneficial gut bacteria. The idea is to starve the yeast by eliminating its primary fuel sources, helping bring Candida levels back under control and reducing those symptoms. One of the most important things you can do on this diet is to load up on non-starchy vegetables like broccoli, spinach, kale, and cauliflower. These veggies not only provide essential nutrients but also help detoxify the body by binding to fungal toxins and carrying them out. For the best nutritional impact, try to eat them raw or lightly steamed. Along with vegetables, getting enough protein is crucial. Good sources include eggs, chicken, turkey, grass-fed beef, and wild-caught fish like salmon, which provide essential amino acids without feeding Candida.

On the flip side, it's important to avoid foods that encourage Candida growth. Sugar, in all its forms—including refined sugar, honey, and agave—should be strictly avoided. Candida thrives on sugar, so cutting it out is key. You can use Stevia as a natural sweetener if you need to since it doesn't spike blood sugar. Processed grains, such as wheat, corn, and barley, also break down into sugars and should be eliminated. Instead, you can occasionally have gluten-free grains like quinoa or buckwheat, but keep these in moderation. When it comes to dairy, especially milk, it's best to avoid it, as it can cause blood sugar spikes. If you really want to include dairy, small amounts of unsweetened yogurt or butter are usually okay.

The length of time you'll need to stick to the Candida diet depends on how severe your overgrowth is. For some, it may just take a few weeks, but in more serious cases, it could mean staying on the diet long-term. Many people also kick off their Candida diet with a cleanse, which helps detoxify the intestines, reduce Candida biofilms (a protective layer Candida forms), and get rid of toxins produced by the yeast.

The Candida diet might also benefit people with conditions like irritable bowel syndrome or leaky gut syndrome. Because it focuses on reducing inflammation, supporting gut health, and fostering the growth of good bacteria, it can help restore balance to the gut microbiome. This, in turn, can lead to better digestion and fewer symptoms associated with these conditions.

That said, the Candida diet isn't without its challenges. It can feel pretty restrictive, and a lot of people struggle with intense sugar cravings as their body adjusts to fewer carbs. It's important to make sure you're still getting enough calories and nutrients, even with the restrictions, to avoid deficiencies. But, as many people discover, once you get into the swing of things, the diet can not only help alleviate Candida-related symptoms but also leave you feeling more energized and in control of your health.

CONNECT WITH DAN

www.yeastinfectionadvisor.com/about-Dan.html
www.facebook.com/people/D-G-Industries-LLC
www.linkedin.com/in/dan-jackowiak-0663761a

ANGELA GODAY: NAVIGATING LIFE'S JOURNEY THROUGH YOGA AND SPIRITUAL TOOLS

Angela Goday's journey is one of resilience, transformation, and the profound healing power of yoga and spirituality. As the founder of Serenity and Salud, Angela is on a mission to guide women towards reclaiming their wellness, cultivating inner calm, and living a life aligned with love. Her personal experience as a Multiple Myeloma survivor has not only shaped her approach to healing but has also inspired her to empower others on their own soul-searching journeys.

In her enlightening chapter, "Feel It to Heal It and Deal With It!", Angela shares her profound insights on how yoga transcends physical flexibility to become a gateway to mental, emotional, and spiritual growth. For Angela, yoga became more than just a practice; it became a lifeline during challenging times, offering solace, self-regulation, and a pathway to personal transformation.

Angela's teachings emphasize the importance of alignment, both on and off the mat. Just as proper alignment in yoga postures protects the integrity of the spine, alignment in life ensures harmony, authenticity, and the free flow of energy. Through yoga, Angela helps individuals reconnect with their intuition, trust their inner wisdom, and realign with their true selves amidst the chaos of modern life.

Moreover, Angela delves into the healing power of breathwork, a fundamental aspect of yoga practice. Breath awareness, she explains, serves as a powerful tool for releasing stress, anxiety, and tension, promoting relaxation, and restoring balance to the mind, body, and spirit. Through simple breathwork exercises, individuals can tap into their innate capacity for self-healing and emotional release.

Angela's spiritual toolkit extends beyond the confines of the yoga mat, encompassing various modalities aimed at promoting holistic well-being. From art therapy to mindfulness practices, from sensory stimulation to transformative travel experiences, Angela encourages individuals to explore diverse paths to healing and self-discovery. Her "Five Senses Self-Soothing Survival Kit" offers a practical approach to managing emotions, fostering inner calm, and navigating life's challenges with resilience and grace.

As Angela aptly states, *"health and wellness are about exploring different paths and keeping them in a mental toolbox or a physical box that you can pull out when you need it."* Through Serenity and Salud, Angela invites women to embark on a journey of self-exploration, self-care, and self-empowerment. Whether through yoga, spiritual practices, or transformative travel experiences, Angela provides the tools, guidance, and support needed to navigate life's journey with courage, grace, and serenity.

When you're ready to embark on your own journey of healing and transformation, visit Serenity and Salud's website to explore Angela's offerings and connect with her on your path to wellness. With Angela's guidance, you can reclaim your wellness, cultivate inner calm, and live a life of serenity and salud.

CONNECT WITH ANGELA

Instagram @serenityandsalud
www.serenityandsaludhangout.com
www.serenityandsalud.com

HANNA'S HALLOWEEN HAUNT

by Hanna Olivas

In the town of ghosts, where shadows play,
Hanna Olivas spooks the night away.
With She Rises Studios, the magic ignites,
Crafting tales that give you frights.

Fenix TV, the screen flickers bright,
Showing witches and goblins that dance in the night.
A cauldron of laughter, a dash of the eerie,
Her stories make you giggle, but also a bit leery.

The pumpkins are grinning, the bats are in flight,
As Hanna spins yarns 'til the first morning light.
So grab your candy, and hold on tight,
It's a funny, spooky Halloween night!

ADRIANA LUNA CARLOS: EMPOWERING WOMEN THROUGH UNWAVERING PERSEVERANCE

Adriana Luna Carlos, a seasoned expert in Web and Graphic design, has embarked on a mission to empower women worldwide through her work at She Rises Studios. With over a decade of experience in the digital arts field, Adriana combines her technical expertise with a passion for helping women overcome insecurities and embrace success.

In her enlightening chapter, "Unwavering Perseverance," Adriana delves into the importance of cultivating resilience and self-understanding in navigating life's challenges. Drawing inspiration from the stories of resilient women, she highlights the transformative power of perseverance in overcoming adversity.

Embracing Challenges:
Adriana encourages women to embrace uncertainties and hurdles as opportunities for personal growth. By reframing challenges as learning experiences, individuals can cultivate resilience and develop the confidence to tackle any obstacle.

Belief in Self:
Through the stories shared in the chapter, Adriana emphasizes the importance of self-belief in overcoming adversity. Women who have triumphed over difficult circumstances did so by believing in themselves and their ability to persevere.

Mindset Shift:
Adriana advocates for a shift in mindset towards positivity and empowerment. By focusing on the good in every situation and maintaining a resilient attitude, women can navigate life's ups and downs with strength and grace.

Empowering Others:
As a podcast host and mentor, Adriana empowers women to take charge of their lives and pursue their dreams. By sharing inspiring stories and providing support, she guides women on a journey of self-discovery and personal growth.

Take the First Step:
Adriana invites readers to take the first step towards empowerment by embracing the stories of triumphant women. Through their experiences, individuals can gain insight and inspiration to overcome obstacles and pursue a fulfilling life.

Changing Perspectives:
By changing the way they perceive challenges, women can unlock their inner strength and resilience. Adriana encourages readers to adopt a positive outlook and approach life's challenges with courage and determination.

As Adriana continues her mission to empower women through unwavering perseverance, she invites individuals to join her in embracing resilience, self-belief, and positivity. Through her work at She Rises Studios and beyond, she is dedicated to helping women rise above obstacles and achieve their full potential.

CONNECT WITH ADRIANA

www.facebook.com/sherisesstudios
www.SheRisesStudios.com

MINDFULNESS AND MENTAL WELL-BEING STRATEGIES

by Gabe Charalambides

Former aerospace engineer Gabe Charalambides is the founder of Odyssey, one of the first providers of legal, professionally guided psilocybin experiences in the United States. He is a mental health and wellbeing advocate and shares his expert insight below in regards to cutting edge mental well-being strategies.

"Psilocybin experiences, when done correctly with guidance, can be a very helpful tool for those who experience an array of issues regarding their mental well-being. When I talk about the effects of psilocybin, the active ingredient in what many know as "magic mushrooms," I want to stress how personal the experience can be. The amount you take, how you're feeling at the moment, and where you are when you take it can shape the experience in many different ways.

Psilocybin invites you to talk about your thoughts, emotions, and even past traumas or deeply buried sadness. I'm not only talking about seeing vivid colors and patterns; it's about confronting and understanding aspects of your mind in ways you might never have without it.

In my practice, we carefully administer psilocybin in safe, controlled settings. We're there to help people navigate their experiences. This careful pairing of psilocybin with psychotherapy has shown promising results. We're learning that it may really improve the therapeutic process, helping to treat various mental health issues.

This technique isn't just about using a psychedelic; it's about understanding yourself through guided introspection and healing. That's the potential power of psilocybin when used responsibly.

Psilocybin has the ability to aid with depression, anxiety, PTSD, and addictions, especially for those who haven't had much luck with traditional methods. Psilocybin can quickly improve mood and improve mental health, much faster than the usual antidepressants that tend to take weeks to kick in.

When participating in psilocybin sessions, you could gain deep insight into your personal thoughts and feelings, which really helps with self-understanding and managing emotions. Plus, it's super helpful in reducing fear responses, providing relief during tough emotional periods. With ongoing efforts to decriminalize and legalize psilocybin in various places, more people are gaining access to it, which increases public interest and research into its benefits.

As experts look into research, the understanding of how psilocybin helps is growing, improving its credibility. On top of that, supportive communities and networks are sprouting up for people using psilocybin for mental wellness, creating a more inclusive environment and shared experiences which is helping to destigmatize this form of wellness."

CONNECT WITH GABE

www.odysseypbc.com
www.linkedin.com/in/gcharalambides

HOW I UNEARTHED MY DHARMA AND BECAME AN ACCIDENTAL AYURVEDA DIGESTIVE HEALTH COACH

by Amayra Morales

Ever since I was a little girl, I've had an insatiable urge to help. Whether it was bringing home injured animals, assisting elderly people across the street, or lending a hand wherever I could, helping others became second nature. By my mid-20s, traveling and volunteering had become the highlights of my adventures. In 2012, I landed a dream job in Laos with an Australian NGO, fulfilling that deep-seated desire. But when my year-long contract ended, I found myself at a crossroads. The fire to help was still burning, but I felt lost on how to channel it.

So, I did what many do when faced with uncertainty—I entered the corporate world as I needed to make ends meet. What I thought would be a temporary detour stretched into a decade. Before I knew it, ten years had flown by, and I found myself hitting rock bottom. One day, I ended up in the hospital, completely burnt out.

I strongly believe that my burnout wasn't due to my stressful job but rather because I was doing something that didn't light me up.

There's nothing quite like staring at the sterile ceiling of a hospital room and asking yourself, "How did I get here?" I had heard of people hitting rock bottom, but I never thought it would happen to me. Yet, there I was, grappling with the realisation that this wasn't a sudden fall—it was a slow, steady accumulation of ignoring all the signs my body had been sending for years.

As strange as it sounds, I'm grateful for that wake-up call from the universe. When I walked out of the hospital, I knew one thing for certain: my time in the corporate world was over.

Within a month, I booked a one-way flight to Bangalore, India, to pursue a dream I had long put on the back burner—Yoga Teacher Training. But not long after I arrived, I got sick again. This time, though, it felt different. I was in a foreign country with no choice but to trust the process and believe I would get better.

Through a series of fortunate events, I found myself in an Ayurveda clinic. That was the turning point. I finally discovered the healing modality that would help me regain my health. After completing my treatment at the clinic, I felt incredible—a sign that I needed to dive deeper into this ancient wisdom. So, I pursued and completed my Master Ayurvedic Digestion and Nutrition certification.

But even then, I wasn't entirely sure what my next step would be. I began sharing what I had learned during my studies, and soon enough, people started reaching out for advice. Then, my cousin said something that changed everything: "Why don't you turn this into a business and get paid for what you're already doing?"

Me, an entrepreneur?
The thought had never crossed my mind, but it made perfect sense. I was truly enjoying helping people improve their health.

And that's how my entrepreneurial journey began. I became an accidental Ayurveda digestive health coach, transforming my passion for healing into a purposeful career.

I now realise that my health challenges were a gift because they forced me to overcome obstacles in order to help others facing similar struggles. My Ayurvedic doctor taught me that health isn't the end goal but rather a vehicle to live your Dharma - your purpose. When you're consumed by health issues, you can lose sight of the bigger picture—that we've all come here to live your best life.

How we do it is through our own unique magic sauce. Now t's time to reconnect with your Dharma.

CONNECT WITH AMAYRA

www.amayramorales.com
www.facebook.com/amayra.r.morales
www.instagram.com/amayra.morales

A JOURNEY TOWARDS SELF-LOVE

by Deborah Corsetti

In the world that demands perfection and comparison, the concept of self-love can be quite difficult. Yet, throughout my journey, I realized that self-love is the foundation in which we can build a life of happiness, fulfillment, and deepen our connection, not only towards others, but most importantly with ourselves.

Embark with me today, on the journey of self-love, where we not only nurture our own well-being, but contribute to the journey towards embracing our own self-worth.

Self love is not just about affirmations and mantras, but it is an absolute necessity for us to build a strong foundation to be able to move through difficult and challenging times in our lives with grace and resilience.

I am a strong advocate for self-love for so many reasons, but here's a few:

Self-love is the basis of fulfilment in our lives. It's recognizing and embracing our unique flaws and all. When we truly love ourselves, we're better equipped to pursue our passions, set goals for ourselves, and cultivate a sense of purpose that resonates from deep within.

Self love isn't just about the self, but it's about how we express ourselves to the world as well. When we love ourselves, we radiate positivity. Self love enables us to be authentic, setting an example for and inspiring those around us, to discover their own journey of self discovery and self acceptance.

When we love ourselves, it is reflected in the way we carry ourselves, the way we speak, and the way we interact with the world. When we love ourselves, we exude confidence and resilience. We become the creators of our reality and draw people and new opportunities towards us .

Loving ourselves is an act of giving not just to ourselves, but to the greater good. When we prioritize our own well-being and happiness, we become better equipped to serve others and make a positive impact on the world around us.

Lastly, I truly believe that self love is the key to empowerment. It allows us to move forward on our journey towards becoming the best versions of ourselves. When we love ourselves unconditionally, we break free from the shackles of self doubts and fear and move towards embracing our own self-worth.

Self-love isn't selfish it's essential!
❀Essential for resilience in challenging moments.
❀Essential for authentic connections.
❀Essential for our emotional well-being and so much more.

Here are some tips for starting YOUR self love journey:

1. Practice self compassion: treat yourself with the same kindness and understanding you would offer to a dear friend. Be gentle with yourself, especially in times of struggle or setback.

2. Practice gratitude: being grateful for the small things that are already in your life can significantly improve your overall well-being. Appreciating the little things in life can lead to greater happiness.

3. Set boundaries: Learn to say no to things that drain your energy or compromise your well-being. Prioritize activities, and relationships that nurse your soul and align with your values.

4. Celebrate your strengths: Embrace your unique talents, skills, and qualities. Celebrate your successes and acknowledge the value you bring to the world.

5. Cultivate mindfulness: Take the time each day to quiet your mind, connect with your breath and tune into the present moment. Practice mindfulness meditation or simply engage in activities that bring you joy and peace.

6. Seek support: Don't be afraid to reach out to friends, family, or a life coach for guidance on your self love journey. Surround yourself with people who uplift and encourage you to be your authentic self.

In conclusion, self-love isn't a luxury… It's a necessity for living a life of fulfillment, happiness, and empowerment.

By prioritizing, our own well-being and fully embracing our worth, we lay the foundation for a brighter, more compassionate world-a world filled with love, acceptance, and endless possibilities. So today, and every day, choose to love yourself completely and unapologetically.

Your journey to self-love starts NOW!

Deb.corsetti on instagram
DCs Mindful Zone on Facebook
DC self guidance on Facebook

A NIGHT TO REMEMBER: THE FENIX TV PREMIER GIFTING SUITE AT THE 76TH ANNUAL EMMYS HOLLYWOOD

The name itself carries a kind of magic, a sense of wonder, nostalgia, and glamour. It's a world where stars shine brightly, where dreams come alive, and where stories that shape cultures and touch hearts are born. This year, during the 76th Annual Emmy Awards, that magic came to life in an unforgettable way. It wasn't just another awards show. No, this year's Emmys was a celebration that transcended the ordinary. It was a return to authentic Hollywood connections, and at the center of it all was FENIX TV's Premier Gifting Suite, an event that was not only a night to remember but one that rekindled the spirit of genuine connection and celebration.

From the moment the plans for this extraordinary night began to take shape, the excitement in the air was electric. We knew that this year would be different—something truly special. The anticipation, the preparation, and the dedication of everyone involved created an energy that was palpable. And when the time came for the FENIX TV Premier

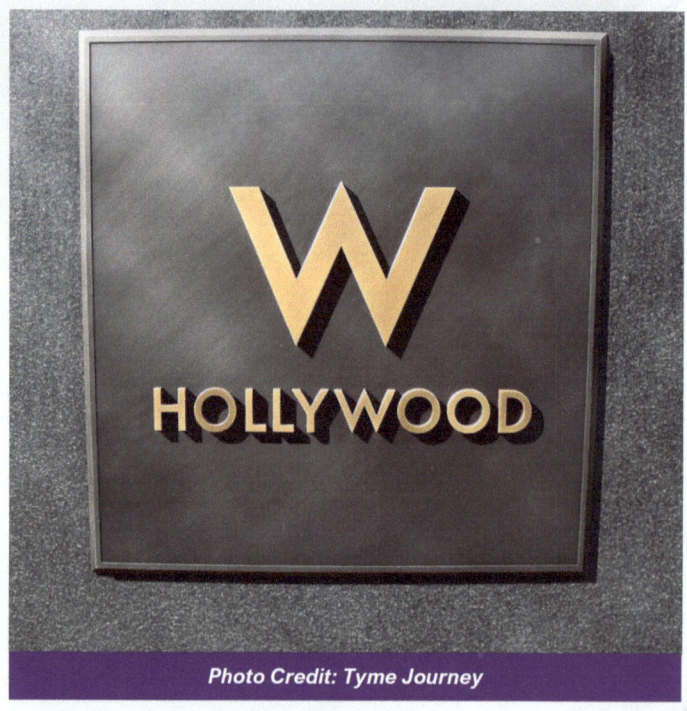

Photo Credit: Tyme Journey

Photo Credit: Tyme Journey

Gifting Suite to open its doors, we were ready to welcome the best of the best from the entertainment industry, offering a night filled with elegance, luxury, and—most importantly—connection.

The W Hollywood Hotel provided the perfect backdrop for this enchanted evening. Its iconic stature in the heart of Hollywood made it

the ideal setting for a night dedicated to celebrating the magic of storytelling and creativity. As guests began to arrive, it was clear that this was going to be an event unlike any other. There was an air of

Photo Credit: Tyme Journey

Photo Credit: Tyme Journey

intimacy, yet also a feeling of grand spectacle. Everyone who walked through those doors wasn't just attending another gifting suite—they were becoming part of a celebration, an experience designed to remind us all of what Hollywood is truly about: connecting, celebrating, and elevating one another.

The red carpet at the FENIX TV Premier Gifting Suite wasn't just a place for photographers to capture stunning images of our guests—it was where magic happened. As each attendee made their way down the carpet, the lights flashed, the cameras rolled, and the energy buzzed with excitement. But it wasn't about the flashing lights or the photoshoots; it was about bringing back what Hollywood has always been known for— the connections. This year, the red carpet was different. There was something genuine in the way people greeted each other, something raw and heartfelt in their interactions. The celebrities, influencers, industry leaders, and creatives who attended weren't just there to be seen; they were there to connect. It was about shaking hands, embracing old friends, and making new ones. It was about the conversations, the laughter, and the stories shared.

Photo Credit: Jared Leighton

Once inside, the night unfolded like a perfectly orchestrated symphony. The Gifting Suite wasn't just a place for attendees to receive luxury items —it was a sensory experience that brought together the best of Hollywood's creativity and generosity. From the moment guests stepped through the doors, they were immersed in an atmosphere that was glamorous yet inviting, opulent yet intimate. Every corner of the

Photo Credit: Jared Leighton

Hanna Olivas, FENIX TV's Chief Branding Officer, took center stage as the Red Carpet Insider for the night. Her presence brought warmth and authenticity to the event, ensuring that each guest felt special and welcomed. Her interviews weren't just about capturing sound bites— they were about celebrating the stories of the people behind the glamour. It was a reminder that behind every star, there is a journey, a story that deserves to be shared.

Photo Credit: Jordan Biagomala

suite was designed to evoke wonder and excitement. Coastal Journeyz, with their luxury beachwear and accessories, offered guests a taste of laid-back elegance, while Corbo Collection, a luxury travel boutique,

Jared Leighton

transported attendees to a world of adventure and indulgence. Every sponsor and gift brought a touch of class and sophistication, offering insights that went beyond material gifts.

Tiffany Harding

Mario Sanchez

Jordan Biagomala

Pure Heavenly Hair Boutique added a dose of beauty and style with their luxury hair and makeup line, making sure each guest felt pampered and polished. The generosity of our sponsors, including Crazy Woman Cellars with their exquisite wine offerings, brought an added layer of enjoyment to the evening. Their commitment to supporting this event was a testament to the power of collaboration and the beauty of giving back. The room was filled with excitement as attendees explored the variety

Tyme Journey

of gifts, from the luxurious to the thoughtful, all curated to create an unforgettable experience. But the FENIX TV Premier Gifting Suite was about more than the gifts. It was about the human connections that were made throughout the night.

David Michael Wyatt, whose soulful voice has captivated audiences around the world, delivered a performance that left everyone in awe. His music was more than just entertainment—it was an emotional

Jeremy Darren Lim

experience that touched the hearts of everyone in the room. Each note he sang seemed to resonate with the very soul of the event, reminding us all why music is such a powerful force in Hollywood and beyond. And then there was DJ Tenn, who kept the energy alive throughout the night with his incredible mixes. His ability to read the room and create a soundtrack that perfectly matched the vibe was nothing short of extraordinary.

Of course, none of this would have been possible without the incredible support of our sponsors and partners. Their belief in the vision of FENIX TV and their commitment to bringing this event to life was the foundation upon which this magical night was built. From the luxurious offerings of

Dyron Pacheco

Coastal Journeyz, Corbo Collection, and Pure Heavenly Hair Boutique to the financial expertise of each sponsor played a pivotal role in making this event an extraordinary success. The W Hollywood Hotel, with its iconic status and impeccable service, provided the perfect setting for the night's festivities. Its glamorous yet intimate atmosphere was the ideal backdrop for an event that was all about connection and celebration. We also want to extend a heartfelt thank you to our incredible photographers and videographers, whose work captured the magic of the night in a way that words could never fully express. Their ability to freeze moments in time—moments of joy, laughter, and connection—ensures that the memories of this night will live on forever.

Jose Peña

Alejandro Martinez

CONNECT WITH US

www.fenixtv.app

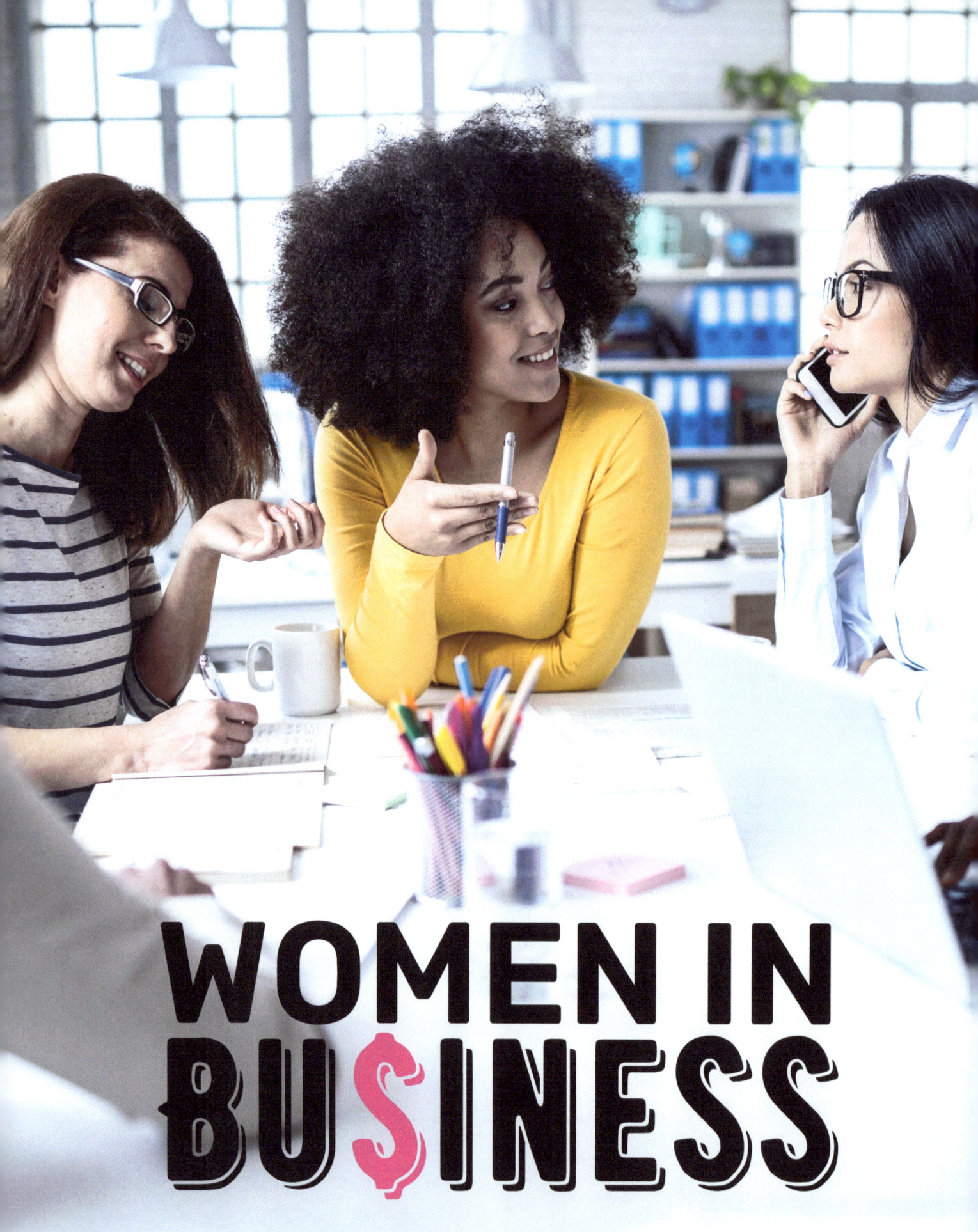

WOMEN IN BU$INESS

EMERGING TRENDS IN HOLISTIC HEALTH AND WELLNESS

by Shanna Bynes Bradford LME, MA, CR

In recent years holistic health and alternative therapies have seen a surge in popularity with physicians, dentistry, licensed medical aestheticians, spa professionals, and holistic practitioners exploring new and innovative products and services to enhance patients' health journeys.

These therapies aim to improve pre- and post-care treatments for both invasive, non-invasive procedures and outpatient surgeries offering a reduced time in healing and beneficial effects for optimal treatment outcomes.

One of the latest trends in holistic health and alternative therapies is the use of aromatherapy. Aromatherapy involves the use of essential oils extracted from plants to promote physical and psychological well-being. These oils can be inhaled or applied to the skin for dermal absorption, providing a range of health benefits. Aromatherapy is known for its air-purifying properties and its ability to enhance relaxation, reduce stress, and improve mood.

Another emerging trend in holistic health is the use of nitric oxide for improving oral health and overall well-being. Nitric oxide is a molecule produced naturally in the body that plays a crucial role in maintaining cardiovascular health, regulating blood pressure, and improving oxygen and blood flow. In the mouth, nitric oxide can help combat harmful microbes and promote oral hygiene. Incorporating nitric oxide into a wellness routine can have a positive impact on overall health by supporting cardiovascular function and circulation.

In addition to aromatherapy and nitric oxide therapy, other trending practices in holistic health include consuming hibiscus tea and tart cherry juice. Hibiscus tea is rich in antioxidants and has been linked to various health benefits, including reducing inflammation, lowering blood pressure, and improving liver health. Tart cherry juice is another popular beverage known for its anti-inflammatory properties and potential to aid in muscle recovery and improve sleep quality. Both hibiscus tea and tart cherry juice can be easily incorporated into a daily wellness routine to support overall health and well-being.

Cryotherapy, or cold therapy, is another emerging trend in holistic health that involves exposing the body to cold temperatures for therapeutic purposes. Cryotherapy has been shown to reduce

Shanna Bynes Bradford LME, MA, CR is an Internationally recognized leading Master Aromatherapist/ Medical Esthetic Educator specializing in dermal absorption of active ingredients and formulating Essential Oil Blends for all parts of the body.

Aside from having more than 25+ years of experience in the Cosmetic, Aesthetic and Beauty industry. Shanna is a Licensed Medical Aesthetician. In the early 2000's Shanna, toured the country with L' Oreal as a National Speaker at "Speaking of Women's Health and the Universal Sister Tour"

inflammation, alleviate pain, and improve athletic performance, skin improvement, hair growth. Topical cryotherapy treatments can provide targeted relief for sore muscles, joint pain, and inflammation, making it a popular choice among athletes and individuals seeking natural pain relief.

Overall, holistic health and alternative therapies continue to gain momentum in the wellness industry as more people seek natural and holistic approaches to health and well-being. From aromatherapy and nitric oxide therapy to hibiscus tea, tart cherry juice, and cryotherapy, these trends offer a wide range of benefits for improving overall health and enhancing the healing process. By incorporating these practices into a holistic wellness routine, individuals can support their physical, mental, and emotional well-being for a more balanced and vibrant life.
As Maya Angelo says, 'when we know better we do better.'

CONNECT WITH SHANNA

@growoutoils

6 SIMPLE STEPS TO HANDLE OVERWHELMING EMOTIONS—YOUR EMOTIONS ARE A RESOURCE

by Fatemeh Farahan, LMFT

Almost every day, I get asked, *"How can I deal with sadness, anger, or that super critical voice in my head?"* If you've ever felt overwhelmed by emotions like these, you're not alone. These feelings can be so intense and uncomfortable that most of us would rather ignore them. But what if I told you there's a better way?

Think of your emotions as a resource—they're not something to avoid or suppress, but signals that help you understand unmet needs. When we learn to listen to our emotions, they can guide us toward healing and growth.

Here's a 6-step system for understanding and managing overwhelming emotions.

1. Pause and Breathe
When an uncomfortable emotion hits, the first thing to do is pause. Stop for a moment and take a deep breath. I recommend the 4-7-8 breathing technique: breathe in for 4 counts, hold for 7, and exhale for 8. This calms your nervous system, giving you space to focus on what's really happening beneath the surface.

2. Label the Emotion
Next, name the emotion. Are you feeling sad? Angry? Anxious? Labeling your emotions helps in several ways:
- It reduces the intensity, creating a little distance from the feeling.
- It engages the reasoning part of your brain, making the emotion easier to manage.
- It improves emotional regulation, helping you respond thoughtfully instead of impulsively.

This step might seem small, but it's scientifically proven to help rewire your brain.

3. Create Space
Once you've labeled the emotion, the next step is to create space between you and the feeling. Imagine standing too close to a painting—you can't see the full picture. When you step back, you get perspective. Similarly, talk to your emotion: "I need a little space to figure out what's going on here." This gives you room to understand what you're feeling.

4. Ask What the Emotion Needs
Emotions are messengers, trying to tell you something important. Ask yourself, *"What is this emotion trying to tell me?"* Maybe anger signals that you need better boundaries, or sadness tells you to rest. Ignoring these messages will only make them louder. Get curious and ask, "What does this emotion need?"

5. Validate the Emotion
Instead of fighting the emotion, validate it. This doesn't mean you're feeding the feeling—it just means acknowledging that it's there for a reason. Think about how great it feels when someone listens to you. Your emotions need that same validation. Once they feel heard, they often calm down.

6. Release and Create Safety with Your Body
Finally, release the emotion physically. Butterfly taps are a simple but powerful technique for this. Cross your arms over your chest like you're hugging yourself, then gently tap your fingers on your upper arms,

alternating left and right, like butterfly wings. This rhythmic tapping helps calm your nervous system and is especially helpful for emotions like sadness or anxiety. Combine this with deep breathing, and you'll feel a real shift in how you experience your emotions.

Final Thoughts
There you have it—6 simple steps to help you manage overwhelming emotions. By treating your emotions as a resource and using both top-down (mind-focused) and bottom-up (body-focused) approaches, you can create balance and safety within yourself. Next time sadness, anger, or frustration comes up, give these steps a try and see how they help.

CONNECT WITH FATEMEH

@farahantherapy

CARING WITHOUT CARRYING: THE ART OF SETTING BOUNDARIES

by Dr. Kiki Ramsey

As a life coach and mental health advocate, I've come to understand the impact that managing mental health through boundaries can have on personal well-being and professional effectiveness. Prioritizing mental health is essential as we navigate the complexities of life. I've developed healthier relationships and environments by fostering self-awareness and recognizing my limits.

Exploring self-care practices like mindfulness and reflection has allowed me to better understand my needs, leading to resilience and emotional stability. One of the crucial realizations in my journey has been the understanding that I cannot care more about someone else's problems than they do. This lesson grew from my deep desire to help others, inspired by my childhood experiences of witnessing my mother's struggles with substance addiction. This later transformed into a mission to support women facing various challenges.

However, as I embarked on my coaching career, I was overly invested in my clients' successes. I often felt a more profound commitment to their goals than they exhibited, which affected my well-being. This dynamic didn't just stay in my professional life; it also carried into my relationships. A significant moment came when a family member contemplated a career change but showed little enthusiasm. Despite their lack of commitment, I became overly involved in their journey, leading me to stress and exhaustion.

During a candid conversation with this family member, I realized the importance of self-efficacy in personal development. I began to understand that while I could provide support and guidance, the responsibility for solving problems ultimately rests with the individual.

Establishing healthy boundaries relieved me. I learned that supporting others does not mean I am responsible for their outcomes. This shift in mindset allowed me to concentrate on areas where I could make an impact, reducing my anxiety and fostering a more favorable environment for both myself and those I aim to help. My journey demonstrates balancing empathy with boundaries, motivating individuals to take ownership of their challenges while protecting my mental well-being.

CONNECT WITH KIKI

www.youtube.com/@DrKikiRamsey
www.instagram.com/drkikiramsey
www.facebook.com/drkikiramsey

ABOUT THE AUTHOR

Dr. Kiki Ramsey is a leading Positive Psychologist, ICF Master Certified Executive Leadership Coach, and founder of the Positive Psychology Coaching and Diversity Institute (PPCaDI), a leadership development firm that specializes in diversity and leadership coaching and training. With a strong background in business, DEI, and positive psychology, Dr. Kiki brings a unique perspective to her work as she helps leaders and organizations create more inclusive and happy work cultures that foster belonging for all. Dr. Kiki also is a Positive Psychology and Coaching professor at Life University.

UNRAVELING DIS-EASE: THE INTRICATE CONNECTION BETWEEN MIND, BODY, AND DISEASE, AND EMPLOYING ESSENTIAL OILS FOR REJUVENATION

by Andrea Bailey-Tweed, CA

In the journey towards holistic health, understanding the intricate relationship between the body and mind is paramount. Our bodies possess an extraordinary ability to communicate with us, often through subtle signals that indicate imbalances or stress. Recognizing these cues and taking proactive steps towards restoration can be transformative. In this article, we explore the fascinating interplay between our bodies and our environment, and explore how essential oils, with their potent therapeutic properties, can aid in restoring balance and vitality to our lives.

Listening to Your Body:

The human body operates as a complex ecosystem, constantly striving for equilibrium. However, the stresses of modern life, coupled with environmental factors, can disrupt this delicate balance, manifesting itself as physical or emotional dis-ease. Symptoms such as fatigue, headaches, digestive issues, or mood fluctuations are not merely random occurrences; they are signals from the body, urging us to pay attention and take action.

Understanding these signals involves tuning into the body's innate wisdom. It requires mindfulness and self-awareness to decipher what our bodies are trying to tell us. Whether it's persistent muscle tension, recurring bouts of anxiety, or unexplained skin irritations, each symptom carries valuable information about our overall well-being.

The Role of Essential Oils:

Essential oils have been used across all cultures and continents for millennia, and have been cherished for their energetic, and therapeutic properties. They offer natural remedies for a myriad of physical and emotional ailments. Distilled from aromatic plants, these concentrated plant extracts contain a rich array of bioactive compounds that interact synergistically with the body, eliciting (resulting in) profound effects on both physiological and psychological levels.

Essential oils are used to support health and well-being. The most common methods of use are via topical application or inhalation. When using a topical application, the essential oil should always be properly diluted (9- 13 drops per half ounce) in a carrier oil. This enables the oils to absorb through the skin and into the blood stream targeting specific areas of pain, muscular discomfort or tension, or other distresses. Inhalation methods include diffusion or direct inhalation by inhaler. This allows the aromatic molecules to penetrate the limbic system of the brain and the respiratory system, influencing mood and promoting relaxation.

Restoring Balance with Essential Oils:

One of the remarkable qualities of essential oils lies in their ability to adapt to the body's needs, exerting balancing effects on multiple levels. For instance, lavender oil, renowned for its calming properties, can soothe frazzled nerves and promote restful sleep. Peppermint oil, with its invigorating aroma, offers relief from headaches and nausea while boosting mental clarity and focus.

ABOUT THE AUTHOR

Andrea spent decades of her life in radio and television broadcasting, along with her top-level work as a communications professional within the United States Government before suffering a health crisis, which led her on a downward spiral. Countless doctor visits, surgeries, and medication were unsuccessful as her health continued to deteriorate. Taking charge of her destiny and health, she employed the power of aromatherapy with miraculous results. Today, she is a certified aromatherapist and founder of Earth's Own Essentials LLC. Her goal is to empower people to be proactive in their health care.

Similarly, oils such as eucalyptus, tea tree, and lemon exhibit potent antimicrobial properties, making them invaluable allies in supporting the immune system and warding off seasonal threats. The gentle floral scent of Chamomile oil can alleviate feelings of tension and anxiety, fostering a sense of tranquility and emotional well-being.

Empowering Wellness:
Incorporating essential oils into daily self-care routines can be a powerful tool for nurturing overall wellness. Whether it is creating a calming atmosphere with a diffuser blend, crafting a soothing massage oil, or formulating a personalized skincare remedy, the possibilities are endless. However, it is important to approach their usage mindfully, respecting their potency and individual properties and following essential oil safety guidelines, particularly when it comes to children.

It is critical when using essential oils to understand that "less is more," but "more is not necessarily better." You do not need more than a few drops of essential oil even if you think you do. These oils are highly concentrated; some use as few as seventy-five pounds of flower to produce a kilo of oil, pure Rose essential oil however, uses 10,000 pounds of rose petals to produce just one pound of essential oils, and there are variations along the way. Key point – essential oils are highly concentrated.

Holistic health encompasses more than just the physical aspect; it encompasses mental, emotional, and spiritual dimensions as well. Cultivating practices such as meditation, yoga, or journaling can complement the therapeutic benefits of essential oils, fostering a deeper connection with oneself and promoting inner harmony.

In the journey towards overcoming dis-ease, our bodies serve as our most trusted guides, offering valuable insights into our well-being. By listening attentively to their signals and embracing the restorative power of essential oils, we can embark on a path of healing and transformation. Let us honor the wisdom of our bodies and harness the gifts of nature to cultivate vibrant health and vitality in every aspect of our lives.

CONNECT WITH ANDREA

www.earthsownessentials.com
www.facebook.com/earthsownessential

FOUR TINY HABITS TO BREAK PROCRASTINATION

by Julie DeLucca-Collin

"Not everything that is faced can be changed. But nothing can be changed until it is faced." — James Baldwin.

I always knew that I wanted to write a book. I have loved writing all my life and figured it would be easy. As I got closer to completing the first few chapters, I started finding reasons not to work on the book It was always so easy to put it off until *"later."* When I submitted my first draft to the editors and got their feedback, my procrastination became ever more pronounced.

We all occasionally put off doing something. When waiting becomes a habit and pattern in our lives, it becomes a problem.

I don't feel like …
I don't want to …
I'll do it tomorrow…

With the demanding and busy lives that many of us women have, these phrases naturally come out of our mouths sometimes! Especially when faced with a challenging task to be done.

Procrastination happens to everyone, even those who are highly productive. Throughout my life, like many business owners, I have been known to suffer from procrastination. In the last few years, however, I have made great strides in overcoming this behavior.

In my journey to become a more productive person, I began to gain the ability to recognize procrastination and the excuses that would creep up from time to time when a deadline was looming. Learning to beat procrastination using a calculated approach that included understanding why I procrastinate. Then, applying strategies to overcome and beat it!

Procrastination is more than just poor time management or laziness. It often comes from negative emotions that keep us hostage from taking action. People put things off because they're not in the right mood. Then they distract themselves with other tasks. Then when they realize their avoidance, feelings of guilt arise for wasting so much time. Your mood worsens because you feel guilty. Your task deadline gets closer. The cycle makes you feel worse.

This continual loop of self-destructive behavior can only be broken when you discover what is causing you to procrastinate.

Most of us experience guilt when we procrastinate. We know what we should do and what's in our best interest, but we struggle to follow through, becoming our own worst enemies.

The trick to beating procrastination is recognizing the habits and patterns that cause you to procrastinate and making changes that stop the behavior, even if difficult at first.

Here are some reasons why you procrastinate and how it can be harmful. I want to dig deeper into recognizing your procrastination habits and patterns and finding ways to halt them.

ABOUT THE AUTHOR

Julie is a highly sought-after TEDx speaker, business coach, and award-winning author dedicated to empowering entrepreneurs and leaders. She has been a corporate speaker at Fortune 50 companies, specializing in women's leadership, confidence, and overcoming imposter syndrome. Julie was the Chief Innovation Officer of a multi-million dollar company in NYC and holds certifications from HarvardX, BerkeleyX, and other prestigious institutions. Her dynamic speaking engagements, workshops, and best-selling book have earned her recognition, including the "25 Most Powerful Minority Women in Business Award" from the Minority Enterprise Executive Council. She also hosts the top-rated podcast *Casa De Confidence*, co-hosting with her husband, inspiring global audiences.

Why Do We Procrastinate?

Fear of failure
- Many people procrastinate because they are afraid of failing. They may feel that if they don't try, they can't fail, so they put off taking action.

Lack of motivation
- When people don't feel motivated to do something, they may procrastinate instead of forcing themselves to take action.

Overwhelm
- When faced with a large or complex task, it can be easy to become overwhelmed and unsure where to start. This can lead to procrastination.

Perfectionism
- People with high standards may procrastinate because they want to do things perfectly. They may feel it's only worth doing something if they can do something perfectly.

Distractions
- In today's world, many distractions can lead to procrastination, such as social media, TV, and video games.

Shortly after completing my book, I knew that I wanted to continue to overcome my procrastinating tendencies. After reading the book Tiny Habits by Dr. BJ Fogg, I became a certified Tiny Habits Coach with the goal of stopping procrastination in its tracks.

The Tiny Habits method is a simple and effective way to break bad habits and create new, positive ones. Developed by BJ Fogg, a behavior scientist at Stanford University, the method involves starting with small, easy-to-do habits that can be built upon over time. Here are the steps to using the Tiny Habits method to overcome procrastination:

How to Use the Tiny Habits Method to Overcome Procrastination

Step 1: Identify the Task You Want to Complete
The first step in using the Tiny Habits method to overcome procrastination is identifying the task you want to complete. This could be anything from writing a report to cleaning the house. Once you have identified the task, break it down into smaller, more manageable steps.

Step 2: Choose a Tiny Habit
Next, choose a tiny habit related to the task you want to complete. This should be something that is easy to do and doesn't take a lot of time. For example, if you want to write a report, your tiny habit could be to write one sentence. If you want to clean the house, your tiny habit could be to put away one item.

Step 3: Anchor the Habit to an Existing Routine
The next step is to anchor your tiny habit to an existing routine. This means choosing a time and place to make your tiny habit that is already part of your daily routine. For example, if you want to write a report, you could write one sentence after opening up your computer for the first time in the morning. If you want to clean the house, you can put away one item whenever you walk into a room.

Step 4: Celebrate Your Success
Finally, celebrate your success every time you complete your tiny habit. This could be as simple as saying "Good job!" to yourself or doing a little happy dance. By celebrating your success, you reinforce the habit and make it more likely that you will continue doing it.

Over time, you can build upon your tiny habit and make it bigger and more challenging. For example, start by writing one sentence and gradually increase to writing a paragraph or a page. By starting small and building up gradually, you will find that you too can overcome procrastination, leading to confidence in all areas of your life.

To learn more about my methods or book a complimentary coffee call, visit: www.goconfidentlycoaching.com

CONNECT WITH JULIE

www.instagram.com/julie_deluccacollins
www.facebook.com/jdelucca
www.tiktok.com/@juliedcbusinesscoach

The SHE RISES STUDIOS PODCAST

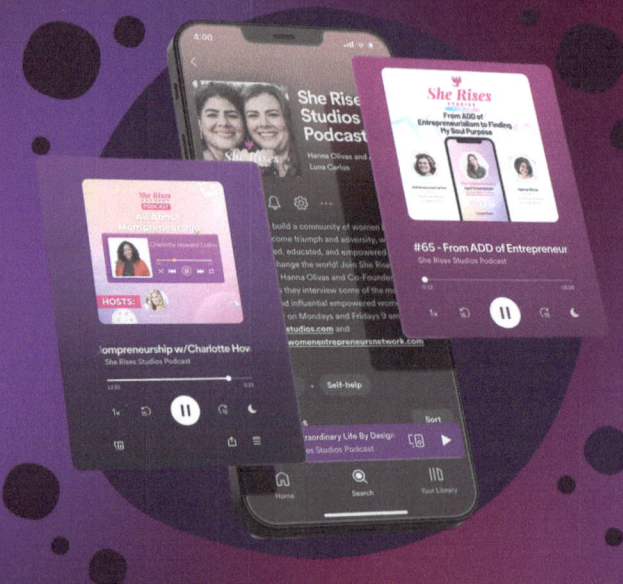

The She Rises Studios podcast is dedicated to empowering women like you to reach their full potential and live their best lives. With inspiring stories, insightful interviews, and practical advice from experts in different industries, our podcast is your go-to source for information, inspiration, and motivation. Join us as we explore topics like:

- Overcoming self-doubt and limiting beliefs
- Building and running a successful business
- Building confidence and Self-esteem
- Navigating career transitions
- Starting and growing a business
- Balancing work and family life
- Improving physical and mental health
- Finding meaning and purpose in life
- So many more

Our guests include successful entrepreneurs, inspiring thought leaders, and everyday women who have overcome challenges and achieved their dreams. Each episode is packed with actionable tips and strategies to help you take your life to the next level.

BREAKING CHAINS: FROM EVENT SUCCESS TO ADDICTION AND BACK

by Connie Paglianiti

I spent over 40 years in the high-pressure world of event management, creating unforgettable experiences with celebrities like Susan Sarandon, Sophia Loren, Jane Seymour and Goldie Hawn. I orchestrated everything from intimate charity galas to large-scale festivals for thousands. My work earned state awards in Victoria, including for the La Dolce Italia Carnevale Masquerade Ball, a finalist for Best New Event. It was a glamorous, fast-paced life. But behind the scenes, I was battling a personal struggle far darker than anyone could have imagined.

From the Pinnacle of Success to Addiction

It all started when a business deal went horribly wrong. I was deceived by someone I trusted, and in an attempt to recover my losses, I turned to gambling. What began as a means to regain control soon spiralled into a destructive addiction. My life, once defined by successful events and accolades, began to unravel.

The losses piled up, not just financially, but emotionally and spiritually. I made choices I deeply regret, choices that ultimately landed me in prison for two and a half years. The shame, guilt, and fear of losing everything I had built were suffocating. When I was released, I isolated myself, spending another two and a half years hiding from the world, convinced my life and career were over.

Rebuilding from the Ashes

Recovery from addiction is never easy, and my journey was no exception. It required humility, vulnerability, and a willingness to face the damage I had done—not just to my life, but to those who trusted me. Through therapy, support groups, and the strength of the people around me, I started to rebuild.

One of the most powerful lessons I learned is that addiction doesn't discriminate. It can take hold of anyone, no matter how successful or in control they may seem. But recovery is possible, and it's worth every moment of struggle. Today, I use my experience to raise awareness about gambling addiction and the importance of breaking the stigma surrounding it.

A New Purpose

In returning to the world of event management, I found a renewed sense of purpose. My career had always been about creating experiences, but now it was about more than just the event itself. It became a platform to champion causes, inspire change, and give back to the communities that supported me.

As a speaker for Gambler's Help and their ReSPIN Program, I share my story to help others avoid the same pitfalls. I want to show people that no matter how far you've fallen, there's always a way back. My story is one of redemption and resilience, and if it can help even one person, it's worth sharing.

I've also channelled my passion for events into educating others. I've written eBooks on event management and developed online courses to train the next generation of event managers. My goal is not just to teach the logistics of running events but to instil the importance of ethics, sustainability, and resilience.

Looking Forward

It's been a long road from award-winning event management to addiction and recovery. The journey has taught me the value of vulnerability, second chances, and self-compassion. I want my story to be a testament to the fact that no matter how deep the fall, you can rise again.

Today, I'm proud of the work I've done and the person I've become. I continue to manage events, speak about addiction recovery, and share my story of resilience.

If my experiences can offer hope and inspiration to others, then every challenge I faced was worth it.

CONNECT WITH CONNIE

www.conniepaglianiti.com
www.linkedin.com/in/conniepaglianiti
www.instagram.com/conniempaglianiti
www.facebook.com/ConniePaglianiti
www.facebook.com/profile.php?id=615603474684477

YOUR INTUITION IS YOUR TREASURE MAP TO HAPPINESS

by Kimberly Beam

One of the things that I have learned over the past couple of years is that human beings are always pressing into what is coming. They are looking for the next thing - sometimes before they even accomplish the now-thing they are working toward.

We move goalposts - move the definition of success further away as we near the goal line. Once we near one milestone, we are looking at the next milestone and forget to celebrate how far we have come and what have done.

Not only are we looking for the next big thing, we get bored easily. We are bored with the same old same, same old. One of the reasons entrepreneurs get into working for themselves is working for somebody else doesn't do that for them anymore or they were never interested in working for somebody else. If we want to be cutting edge, if we want to be innovative, if we want to be doing something completely new, we need to be stepping out and stepping into our intuition.

Albert Einstein says imagination is more important than knowledge. He knew that E=MC2 before it was proven, and it took the experimental physicists to prove what he knew theoretically. He used his brain and his imagination to come up with something brand new.

We as regular human beings have to press into what is new and exciting for us to feel alive at our positions. Often we feel stuck doing the tasks we don't love - and for me that's emails and social media posts and compiling my podcast. This is not fun for me. However, what is more fun for me and what does light me up is pressing into my intuition for other people, being able to hear words that encourage inspire uplift, give direction and hope - this is the foundation of the work I choose to focus on. If in your business you're feeling you are only swimming in the mediocre, the humdrum, like you're being bogged down by the nitty-gritty day-to-day, I encourage you to step out and into a space where you allow your imagination to be free.

Where are you most alive? Is that at the beach? Is that in the woods? Is that in a room in your house? Is that at your child's game? At the gym? In a yoga studio? Where do you feel most allowed to be imaginative, excited, and free to dream?

It is in those dreaming spaces where you allow your mind time to think. I encourage you to find ways to give your brain space to be creative and

imaginative. Our brains need the opportunity to percolate and breathe in order to create new ideas and allow for room to pull ideas together that inspire exciting vision and direction for where you are, where you want to be, and how to get there.

In my work with individuals, I teach them not only how to get in touch with their body and their intuition, but how to also dream and explore. We are not born with a physical treasure map of where to find in our happiness and our joy. However, there is an internal guidance system within and around you, that when you learn how to tap into that, you are rarely uncertain of how to steer the ship of your life.

You are the captain of the ship and the master of your destiny. Your intuition is the "treasure map", the guide, and when you learn how to read that map - you learn how your intuition speaks to you - you are being steered by your higher purpose and dreams.

KIM BEAM

THE WAY TO CREATE THE LIFE YOU LOVE IS THROUGH MEDITATION AND INTUITION. LET ME SHOW YOU HOW.

BYE, BYE, BUNIONS! HOW LAPIPLASTY® 3D BUNION CORRECTION® IS TRANSFORMING BUNION TREATMENT

by Brad Schaeffer, DPM

As a board-certified foot and ankle specialist, I have been treating a variety of podiatric ailments for more than 10 years. Patients arrive at my office suffering from warts, bone spurs and hammertoes, but one of the most common and painful conditions they experience is bunions. Whether patients spend their weekends running marathons or just walking around their neighborhoods, bunions can impact almost any part of their daily routines. For decades, patients with bunions often avoided getting them corrected because of the reputation associated with traditional treatment options. I am pleased to be part of a growing number of specialists offering a procedure that uses a unique approach to address this painful and progressive condition—Lapiplasty® 3D Bunion Correction®.

Many people with bunions are surprised to learn how common the condition is. The deformity affects almost 25% of American adults. Nonsurgical options such as shoe inserts and splints may provide patients with temporary relief from their bunion pain, but the only way to correct the deformity is with surgery. For more than 30 years, this involved shaving the protruding bone on the side of the toe without addressing the root cause of the deformity. The Lapiplasty® Procedure allows physicians to correct the condition at its root cause using a system of innovative titanium plates to secure the unstable joint in the foot[5],[6]. Many patients can put weight on their affected foot while wearing a walking boot within weeks after surgery and most can return to physical activities within about four months. The procedure has demonstrated a low risk of recurrence, with 97% and 99% of patients maintaining their 3D corrections in studies at 13- and 17-months post-op, respectively. Since the procedure was cleared by the FDA in 2016, more than 100,000 patients have chosen the Lapiplasty® Procedure to allow them to enjoy life bunion-free.

Many of my patients suffering from bunions arrive at my office with fear that their feet will never feel better. I am grateful to be able to offer them an option that can allow them to get back on track towards returning to the lifestyles they once enjoyed.

For more information about the Lapiplasty® Procedure™, visit **www.Lapiplasty.com**.

Only a surgeon can tell if the Lapiplasty® Procedure is right for you. This experience is unique and specific to this patient only. Individual results may vary depending on age, weight, health, and other variables. There are risks and recovery takes time. For more information about recovery from the Lapiplasty® Procedure, see the recovery information and discuss the post-surgery recovery process with your doctor. Risks include infection, pain, implant loosening and loss of correction with improper bone healing. For more information on benefits, risks and recovery, visit **Lapiplasty.com**.

TMC Inc. does not recommend any particular surgeon. Patients should make an independent determination regarding the qualifications of suitability of Lapiplasty surgeons found at **Lapiplasty.com/doctor**.

ABOUT THE AUTHOR

Dr. Brad Schaeffer is a board-certified foot and ankle surgeon who practices in New York City, Piscataway, NJ and Hillsborough Township, NJ. He completed a three-year comprehensive foot and ankle reconstructive surgical residency after graduating from medical school and now treats a wide range of conditions. When he isn't busy treating patients at his practice and on TLC's hit show, My Feet are Killing Me, Dr. Schaeffer enjoys exercising and spending time with his family.

FROM ADDICTED AND ABUSED TO A BEAUTIFUL BLESSING

by Teri Katzenberger

A Walk in My Shoes

Having self-image issues and a health altering eating disorder for more than 20 years, as well as other serious life altering addictions and challenges, I can certainly relate to most individuals.

On my own personal health and wellness journey since 1991, I teach and train people everything I currently do, and have done, to live a healthy, clean, full active life!

More people today, than ever before, want to feel good - look good and most importantly, live a healthy life. They do not want to be held hostage by their scale nor in bondage to health issues and ailments.

Finding the Way...

In 1991, I became a divine overcomer of entities that were meant to kill me. At the age of 23, I left a grossly abusive marriage. I overcame a chronic drug and alcohol addiction. I overcame a chronic dual eating disorder.
That is when my own personal journey of health, body wellness, fitness and nutrition began. I was on a journey to save my own life!

Hello World! I'm Teri Katzenberger. I am the founder and owner of the Live Well Now Academy LLC.

I started my journey as an Entrepreneur in the Health and Lifestyle Wellness industry in 2000. I have dedicated myself to helping people live a healthy, well, fit, strong, whole life from the inside out; without fad dieting and unrealistic expectations.

My Moto: *"We certainly age each year; however, we do NOT have to grow old in the process!"*

In 2000, God chose me to teach, educate and help others live a healthy, well, fit, strong, whole life from the inside out.

I have a Certification Specialization in Medical Fitness and Hormone Fitness. I also earned a degree in Fitness and Nutrition as well as a degree in Business Administration. I have numerous Certifications as a Transformation Life Coach, Life Story Coach, Sobriety Life Coach, Mindfulness Coach, Group and Circuit Training and Personal Development Training, and many more!

As life evolves, I believe in ongoing education. I don't believe in a *"one size fits all"* nor do I have a cookie cutter approach. We are all different makes and models shapes and sizes. Every *"Body"* is different.

Since 2005 I have been a Functional Health and Lifestyle Wellness Practitioner. I specialize in people. Your healthy results are my Specialty. People matter to me. Their life matters to me. Their future self, matters to me.

Since 2017 I have been on my own personal journey once AGAIN! I began battling with disabling depression and paralyzing anxiety. By the time 2020-2021 rolled around I was a hot mess. I truly thought I was going to have a mental break down or remove myself from this thing called life. I was watching my in-person Fitness and Lifestyle Wellness Center deteriorate.

One morning in August 2021, when I was sipping my coffee and watching a Hallmark Movie, the Holy Spirit whispers *"It's O.K. to get through what you're going through"*. I exhaled, fell back into my lazy boy and received that message three more times. I KNEW exactly what those words meant!

As women, we are led to believe that something is "wrong with us" if we show emotions. If we become emotional. We try to figure out *"what is wrong with me. Why am I feeling the way I am"?* Sometimes…It is nothing. It's just how we feel!

Feelings aren't right or wrong, they just are. And THAT is O.K. From that moment forward I continue to share my journey with people – sharing; *"It's O.K. to get through what you're going through"*!

CONNECT WITH TERI

www.livewellnowacademy.club
www.livewellnowacademy.com
www.facebook.com/TeriKatzenberger
www.instagram.com/terikatzenberger
www.linkedin.com/in/livewellnow

JOIN OUR COMMUNITY

We believe the future is female and that we are better and stronger together. This group is NOT just for entrepreneurs but for women in general of all ages and from all walks of life.

www.bit.ly/srscommunitygroup

WE ARE
SHE RISES STUDIOS

We are a real-life community of women working to become the best version of themselves to change their lives and make the world a better place.

Group by **Hanna J Olivas**

She Rises Studios Community

🔒 Private group · 6.4K members

    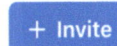 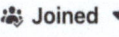   ＋ Invite   ↗ Share   👥 Joined ⌄   ⌄

Discussion   Featured   Members   Events   Media   Files   🔍   ···

⬤ Write something...   **About**

www.ingramcontent.com/pod-product-compliance
Lightning Source LLC
Chambersburg PA
CBHW041731140626
46547CB00025BA/182

* 9 7 8 1 9 6 4 6 1 9 5 7 6 *